Awards of Attorneys Fees by Federal Courts, Federal Agencies and Selected Foreign Countries

AWARDS OF ATTORNEYS FEES BY FEDERAL COURTS, FEDERAL AGENCIES AND SELECTED FOREIGN COUNTRIES

MARY V. CAPISIO (EDITOR)

Novinka Books
New York

Senior Editors: Susan Boriotti and Donna Dennis
Coordinating Editor: Tatiana Shohov
Office Manager: Annette Hellinger
Graphics: Wanda Serrano
Editorial Production: Jennifer Vogt, Matthew Kozlowski and Maya Columbus
Circulation: Ave Maria Gonzalez, Indah Becker, Raymond Davis
and Vladimir Klestov
Communications and Acquisitions: Serge P. Shohov

Library of Congress Cataloging-in-Publication Data
Available Upon Request

ISBN 1-59033-246-6

400 Oser Ave, Suite 1600
Hauppauge, New York 11788-3619
Tele. 631-231-7269 Fax 631-231-8175
e-mail: Novascience@earthlink.net
Web Site: http://www.novapublishers.com

Printed in the United States of America

CONTENTS

PREFACE

This book discusses in details assorted statutory exceptions and acts that have been enacted to encourage on equalization of law among private parties and bureaucratic and governmental entities. There is an emphasis given to the American Civil Rights cause, taxation and consumer and environmental protection cases when dealing with assorted attorneys' fees provisions. Measures such as the Equal Access to Justice Act which allows rewards against the U.S. Government despite the fact that the American rule bars the U.S. from the payment of attorneys' fees; and the reimbursement of attorneys' fees using the Independent Counsel Law which was under the common law perhaps most apparent during the Iran-Contra Investigation. Also dealt with here is the Fair Access to Indemnity and Reimbursement Act, the Taxpayer Bill of Rights 3 enacted under the IRS Restructuring and Reform Act of 1998 and a complete listing of state attorneys' fees agreements in the U.S. concerning State tobacco litigation cases. In addition, a recording of attorneys' fees lawmaking from assorted countries is provided concerning contingency fee arrangements, the liability for litigation expenses, the regulation of attorneys' fees in civil litigation and the existence of any given reform proposals.

Chapter 1

AWARDS OF ATTORNEYS' FEES BY FEDERAL COURTS AND FEDERAL AGENCIES

Henry Cohen

INTRODUCTION: THE AMERICAN RULE AND ITS EXCEPTIONS

"In the United States, the prevailing litigant is ordinarily not entitled to collect a reasonable attorneys' fee from the loser." *Alyeska Pipeline Service Co. v. Wilderness Society,* 421 U.S. 240,247 (1975). This is known as the "American rule" (as opposed to the English rule, which routinely permits fee-shifting) and derives from court-made law. It has, however, numerous statutory exceptions (listed at the back of this report) some, if not most, of which Congress enacted in order to encourage private litigation to implement public policy. *Id.* at 263. Under these exceptions, a federal court (and sometimes a federal agency) may order the losing party to a lawsuit to pay the winning party's attorneys' fees. Although "attorney's fees generally are not a recoverable cost of litigation 'absent explicit congressional authorization,' ….. [t]he absence of specific reference to attorney's fees is not dispositive if the statute otherwise evinces an intent to provide for such fees."[1]

---

1 Key Tronic Corp. v. United States, 511 U.S. 809, 814-815 (1994) (holding that the phrase "any other necessary costs of response incurred by any other person" in § 107 of the Comprehensive Environmental Response, Compensation, and Liability Act, 42 U.S.C. § 9607, does not include attorneys' fees).

Fee-shifting has been proposed, not only to encourage lawsuits, but to discourage them, especially tort suits. The English "loser pays" rule was included in tort reform legislation proposed by the Bush Administration in 1992, and in "The Common Sense Legal Reforms Act," which is part of the "Contract With America" proposed by the Republican House Members in 1994.[2]

The American rule has two major common law exceptions (instances when federal courts may award attorneys' fees without statutory authorization): the common benefit doctrine and the bad faith doctrine.[3] These derive from the historic authority of the courts "to do equity in a particular situation."[4] This authority has been called the "supervisory" or "inherent" power of the federal courts.[5]

Federal courts may use this inherent power even in diversity cases, which are cases arising under state law that are brought in federal court pursuant to 28 U.S.C. § 1332 when the parties are citizens of different states and the amount in controversy exceeds $50,000. *Chambers v. NASCO, Inc.,* 501 U.S. 32 (1991). In *Alyeska,* the Court had written that, "in the ordinary diversity case where the state law does not run counter to a valid federal statute or rule, of court, and usually it will not, state law denying the right to attorney's fees or giving right thereto, which reflects a substantial policy of the state, should be followed." 421 U.S. at 259 n.31. In *Chambers,* the Court explained that this limitation "applies only to fee-shifting rules that embody a substantive policy, such as a statute which permits a prevailing party in certain classes of litigation to recover fees." 501 U.S. at 52. A substantive policy of the state is not "implicated by the assessment of attorney's fees as a sanction for bad-faith conduct before the court which involved disobedience of the court's orders and the attempt to defraud the court itself." *Id.* at 52-53.

---

2 *See, Attorneys Fees: The Bush Administration Proposal to Adopt the English Rule* (CRS Report No. 92-237 A, Feb. 28, 1992); *Common Sense Legal Reforms Act of 1995: Title I — Civil Justice Reform (Attorneys' Fees, Products Liability, Etc.)* (CRS Report No. 95-27 A, Jan. 24, 1995). The Attorney Accountability Act of 1995, H.R. 988, 104th Cong., which grew out of the Common Sense Legal Reforms Act of 1995, passed the House.

3 The Supreme Court has noted a third exception: "a court may assess attorney's fees as a sanction for the 'willful disobedience of a court order.'" Chambers v. NASCO, Inc., 501 U.S. 32, 45 (1991). However, this may be viewed as falling within the bad faith doctrine.

4 Sprague v. Ticonic National Bank, 307 U.S. 161, 166 (1939).

5 *See,* United States v. Horn, 29 F.3d 754, 759 (1st Cir. 1994) (sovereign immunity precludes use of supervisory power to order the United States to pay the fees and costs incurred by criminal defendants in litigating prosecutorial misconduct issue; *but see,* Public Law 105-119 (1997), discussed at pp. *59-60, infra).* Although the Supreme Court noted in *Chambers, supra* note 3, 'That the exercise of the inherent power of lower federal courts can be limited by statute or rule, for '[t]hese courts were created by act of Congress"' (501 U.S. at 47; the Supreme Court was created by the Constitution, Art. III, § I), the court of appeals in *Horn* wrote: "It is not yet settled whether some residuum of the courts' supervisory power is so integral to the judicial function that it may not be regulated by Congress (or, alternatively, may only be regulated up to a certain point)." 29 F.3d at 760 n.5.

COMMON LAW EXCEPTIONS TO THE AMERICAN RULE

Common law exceptions to the American rule are "unquestionably assertions of inherent power in the courts to allow attorneys' fees in particular situations, unless forbidden by Congress." *Alyeska,* 421 U.S. at 259. The two major exceptions are cases in which a party at its own expense creates a fund or achieves a substantial benefit in which others share, and cases in which a party acts in bad faith. A former third exception, cases in which a plaintiff acts as a "private attorney general" in effectuating important public policy, was eliminated by the Supreme Court in *Alyeska.*

Common Benefit Doctrine

"In the absence of a statutory prohibition, the federal courts have authority to award attorneys' fees from a fund to a party who, having a common interest with other persons, maintains a suit for the common benefit and at his own expense, resulting in the creation or preservation of a fund, in which all those having the common interest share." Annotation, 8 L.Ed.2d 894, 905 (1963). This exception to the American rule does not shift the cost of attorneys' fees to the losing party, but rather to those who benefit from the suit. The doctrine was originally conceived in *Trustees v. Greenough,* 105 U.S. 527 (1881), a case against trustees often or eleven million acres of land who had collusively sold hundreds of thousands of those acres at nominal prices. One beneficiary, after eleven years of litigation at his own expense, recaptured the assets and presented a claim for reimbursement of attorneys' fees. The Supreme Court approved the award, writing that "if the complainant is not a trustee, he has at least acted the part of a trustee in relation to the common interest." *Id.* at 532.

In *Mills v. Electric Auto-Lite* Co., 396 U.S. 375, 392 (1970), the Supreme Court held that under the common benefit doctrine there is no requirement "that the suit actually bring money into the court as a prerequisite to the court's power to order reimbursement of expenses." *Mills* was a stockholders' derivative suit, a type of case which, the Court noted, may bring substantial non-pecuniary benefits.

Boeing Co. v. Van Gemert, 444 U.S. 472 (1980), was a successful class action in which over $3 million in damages were awarded. Some class members collected their shares of the damages, but others did not. The district court, invoking the common benefit doctrine, ordered that the plaintiffs' attorneys be awarded their fees from the total amount of the judgment, concluding that it was equitable for all class members claiming and non-claiming alike — to bear *a pro rata* share of the costs of producing the judgment in their favor. The defendant objected to use of the unclaimed money for this purpose, arguing that the ultimate disposition of the unclaimed money had not been decided. But the Supreme Court affirmed the award of attorneys' fees, holding:

> The common-fund doctrine, as applied in this case, is entirely consistent with the American rule against taxing the losing party with the victor's attorney's fees.... Boeing presently has no interest in any part of the fund. Any right that Boeing may establish to the return of the money eventually claimed is contingent on the failure of the absentee class members to exercise their present rights of possession. Although Boeing itself cannot be obliged to pay fees awarded to the class lawyers, its latent claim against unclaimed money in the judgment fund may not defeat each class member's equitable obligation to share the expenses of litigation.

Id. at 481-482.

Bad Faith Exception

In *Hall v. Cole,* 412 U.S. 1, 5 (1973), the Supreme Court wrote:

> [I]t is unquestioned that a federal court may award counsel fees to a successful party when his opponent has acted 'in bad faith, vexatiously, wantonly, or for oppressive reasons....' In this class of cases, the underlying rationale of 'fee shifting' is, of course, punitive, and the essential element in triggering the award of fees is therefore the existence of 'bad faith' on the part of the unsuccessful litigant.

A fee award under the bad faith exception requires subjective bad faith— "some proof of malice entirely apart from inferences arising from the possible frivolous character of a particular claim." *Copeland v. Martinez,* 603 F.2d 981, 991 (D.C. Cir. 1979), *cert. denied,* 444 U.S. 1044 (1980).

In *Hall v. Cole,* the Supreme Court wrote: "It is clear.... that 'bad faith' may be found, not only in the actions that led to the lawsuit, but in the conduct of the litigation." 412 U.S. at 15. Subsequently, as another court wrote: "Federal courts have applied [the bad faith] exception both when bad faith occurred in connection with the litigation and when it was an aspect of the conduct that gave rise to the lawsuit."[6] However, some courts have refused to apply the bad faith exception to a party's underlying claim, noting that the Supreme Court's statement in *Hall v. Cole* had concerned the common benefit exception, not the bad faith exception.[7]

---

6 Nepera chemical, Inc. v. Sea-Land Service, 794 F2d 688, 701 (D.C. Cir. 1986).

7 *See, e.g.,* Sanchez v. Rowe, 870 F.2d 291, *295* (5th Cir. 1989) ("We hold that the requisite bad faith may be found in a party's conduct in response to a substantive claim, whether before or after the action is filed, but it may not be based on a party's conduct forming the basis for that substantive claim" (emphasis in original)). In *Shimrnan v. International Union of Operating Engineers,* 744 F.2d 1226, 1231 (6th Cir. 1984) (en banc), *cert. denied,* 469 U.S. 1215 (1985), the court wrote: "To allow an award of attorneys' fees based on bad faith in the act underlying the substantive claim would not be consistent with the rationale behind the American Rule regarding attorneys' fees. ...Attorneys' fees incurred while curing the original wrong are not compensable because they represent the cost of maintaining open access to an equitable system of justice." Attorneys' fees incurred as the result of

An attorney, as well as a party, who acts in bad faith may be ordered to pay the attorneys' fees of the opposing party. In *Roadway Express, Inc. v. Piper,* 447 U.S. 752, 765-767 (1980), the Supreme Court held:

> [I]n narrowly defined circumstances federal courts have inherent power to assess attorney's fees against counsel... . The power of a court over members of its bar is at least as great as its authority over litigants. If a court may tax counsel fees against a party who litigated in bad faith, it certainly may assess those expenses against counsel who willfully abuse judicial processes... . Like other sanctions, attorney's fees certainly should not be assessed lightly or without fair notice and an opportunity for a hearing on the record. But in a proper case, such sanctions are within a court's powers.

In Durrett v. Jenkins Brickyard, Inc., 678 F.2d 911, 919 (11th Cir. 1982), the court held "that the Court in *Roadway Express* intended to authorize the assessment of attorney's fees against counsel who either willfully disobeyed a court order or acted in bad faith, vexatiously, wantonly, or for oppressive reasons."

In *Roadway Express,* the Supreme Court also noted that, under Federal Rule of Civil Procedure 37(b), "[b]oth parties and counsel may be held personally liable for expenses, 'including attorney's fees caused by the failure to comply with discovery orders." 447 U.S. at 763. The Court also found that only excess costs, not attorneys' fees, could be assessed under 28 U.S.C. § 3927, which provided that any attorney "who so multiplies the proceedings in any ease so as to increase costs unreasonably and vexatiously may be required by the courts to satisfy personally such excess costs." However, the section soon after was amended by Public Law 96-349, § 3, to permit awards of attorneys' fees as well as excess costs against counsel.[8]

Private Attorney General Doctrine

The private attorney general doctrine provides that a plaintiff "should be awarded attorneys' fees when he has effectuated a strong Congressional policy which has benefited a large class of people, and where further the necessity and financial burden of private enforcement are such as to make the award essential."[9] Many of the statutory exceptions to the American rule are based on this concept. In *Newman v.*

---

bad faith in the conduct of the litigation, however, are compensable because such bad faith constitutes a new wrong imposed upon the aggrieved party.

8 Cases under 28 U.S.C. § 1927 are discussed at 12 ALR Fed 910. Other cases concerning the bad faith exception to the American rule are discussed at 31 ALR Fed 833.

9 La Raza Unida v. Volpe, 57 F.R,D. 94, 98 (N.D. Cal. 1972), *aff'd,* 488 F.2d 559 (9th Cir. 1973), *cert. denied,* 417 U.S. 968 (1974).

Piggie Park Enterprises, Inc., 390 U.S. 400, 402 (1968), the Supreme Court, discussing one such exception, wrote:

> If successful plaintiffs were routinely forced to bear their own attorneys' fees, few aggrieved parties would be in a position to advance the public interest by invoking the injunctive power of the federal courts. Congress therefore enacted the provision for counsel fees... to encourage individuals injured by racial discrimination to seek judicial relief under Title II [42 U.S.C. § 2000a-3(b)].

Prior to the Supreme Court's decision *in Alyeska,* some lower federal courts had awarded attorneys' fees under the private attorney general doctrine in suits brought under statutes that had no fee-shifting provisions, thereby creating another court-made exception to the American rule. *Alyeska* at 270 n.46. In *Alyeska,* however, the Court held:

> [C]ongressional utilization of the private attorney general concept can in no sense be construed as a grant of authority to the Judiciary to jettison the traditional rule against non-statutory allowances to the prevailing party and to award attorneys' fees whenever the court deems the public policy furthered by a particular statute important enough to warrant the award.

421 U.S. at 263.

The primary reasons the Court gave for its decision were the difficulty "for the courts without legislative guidance to consider some statutes important and some unimportant" and the fact that "the rational application of the private-attorney-general rule would immediately collide with the express provision of 28 U.S.C. § 2412," which at the time prohibited fee awards against the United States, except when specifically permitted by statute. *Id.* at 263 -266.

Congress' immediate response to *Alyeska* was enactment of the Civil Rights Attorney's Fees Awards Act of 1976,42 U.S.C. § 1988(b), which is discussed at page 33.[10] Congress has since enacted many more statutes that authorize awards of attorneys' fees in specific situations, but it has not reversed *Alyeska* to grant courts the power to award attorneys fees to private attorneys general in cases brought under statutes that do not provide for fee-shifting.

---

[10] When enacted in 1976, this statute was codified as the last sentence of 42 U.S.C. § 1988. In 1991, Public Law 102-166, § 113(a), made it a separate subsection. For simplicity, it is referred to throughout this report (except in quotations) as § 1988(b), even when discussing court decisions between 1976 and 1991, when it was the last sentence of § 1988.

THE EQUAL ACCESS TO JUSTICE ACT

Awards of attorneys' fees against the United States were barred at common law not only because of the American rule, but also because of the doctrine of sovereign immunity, under which the United States may not be sued, nor its funds expended, without its consent. "Congress alone has the power to waive or qualify that immunity,"[11] and it did so, with respect to awards of attorneys' fees, with the Equal Access to Justice Act (EAJA) in 1980. Prior to enactment of EAJA, the common law exceptions to the American rule were inapplicable against the United States.[12] Even statutory exceptions to the American rule were inapplicable against the United States unless they specifically authorized fee awards against the United States.

EAJA allows awards of attorneys' fees against the United States in two broad situations. The first, codified at 28 U.S.C. §2412(b), makes the United States liable for the prevailing party's attorneys' fees to the same extent that any other party would be under the common law and statutory exceptions to the American rule, including the statutory exceptions that do not specifically authorize fee awards against the United States. This provision, unlike the rest of EAJA, contains no limitations on the assets or number of employees of parties eligible to recover fees, and no maximum hourly rate for fee awards.

The second broad situation in which EAJA authorizes fee awards against the United States is codified at 5 U.S.C. §504 and 28 U.S.C. §2412(d). These sections provide that, in specified agency adjudications[13] and in all civil actions (except tort actions and tax cases)[14] brought by or against the United States, the United States shall

---

11 United States v. Chemical Foundation, Inc., 272 U.S. 1, 20 (1926).

12 *See, e.g.,* National Association of Regional Medical Health Programs. Inc. v. Mathews, 551 F.2d 340 (D.C. Cir. 1977), *cert. denied,* 431 U.S. 954 (1977) (common benefit exception); Gibson v. Davis, 587 F.2d 280 6th Cir. 1978). *cert. denied,* 441 U.S. *905* (1979) (bad faith exception).

13 The type of agency adjudication in which fees may be awarded is an "adversary adjudication," which is defined at 5 U.S.C. § 504(b)(l)(C). *In Ardestani v. Immigration and Naturalization Service,* 502 U.S. 129 (1991), the Supreme Court held that administrative deportation proceedings are not adversary adjudications. In *Sullivan v. Hudson,* 490 U.S. 877, 891 (1989), the Supreme Court held "that for purposes of the EAJA Social Security benefit proceedings are not 'adversarial' within the meaning of § 504(b)(1)(C) either initially or on remand from a court." However, "where a court orders a remand to the Secretary [of Health and Human Services] in a benefits litigation and retains continuing jurisdiction over the case pending a decision from the Secretary which will determine the claimant's entitlement to benefits, the proceedings on remand are an integral part of the 'civil action' for judicial review and thus attorney's fees for representation on remand are available [under 28 U.S.C. § 2412(d)(1)(A)] subject to the other limitations in the EAJA." *Id.* at 892. *See,* 96 ALR Fed 336.

Social Security eases also raise complications in applying the EAJA's requirement that the prevailing party submit a fee application "within thirty days of the final judgment in the action" (28 U.S.C. § 2412(d)(l)(B)) or "within thirty days of a final disposition in the adversary adjudication" (5 U.S.C. § 504(a)(2)). *See,* Melkonyan v. Sullivan, 501 U.S. 89 (1991); Shalala v. Schaefer, 509 U.S. 292 (1993).

14 The EAJA applies in all Article III courts *(see,* 28 U.S.C. § 24 12(c)), and explicitly applies in two Article I courts: the Court of Federal Claims and the United States Court of Veterans Appeals (28 U.S.C. § 2412(d)(2)(F)). As for other Article I courts, it does not apply in Tax Court (Bowen v.

be liable for the attorneys' fees of prevailing parties, unless it proves that its position was substantially justified or that special circumstances make an award unjust.[15]

This second portion of EAJA contains two limitations on fee awards that are not found in § 2412(b).[16] First, it prescribes a fee cap unless the court or agency determines that a special factor justifies a higher fee. (Most fee statutes authorize awards of "reasonable" fees, with the amount determined by the court). The cap was originally $75 per hour, but Public Law 104-121, §§ 231-233, increased it to $125 per hour for cases commenced on or after the date of its enactment, which was March 29, 1996. Second, this portion of EAJA does not allow (with two exceptions) fees to be awarded to individuals whose net worth exceeds $2 million, or to businesses or organizations, including units of local government, with a net worth exceeding $7 million or more than 500 employees.[17] This portion of EAJA sunset, by the terms of the original Act, on October 1, 1984. In 1985, EAJA was reenacted, retroactive to October 1, 1984, and made permanent.

Public Law 104-121, in addition to raising the cap under EAJA to $125 per hour, added the following provision to 28 U.S.C. § 2412(d), and a corresponding one to 5 U.S.C. § 504 applicable to adversary adjudications:

Commissioner, 706 F.2d 1087 (1lth Cir. 1983)); with respect to tax cases, *see,* p. 38 of this report). In addition, "[t]he circuits are divided about whether bankruptcy courts are 'courts of file United States' and therefore have authority under EAJA or [26 U.S.C.] section 7130 *in re* Cascade Roads, Inc., 34 F.3d 756, 767 n.12 (9th Cir. 1994). See, Charles R. Haywood, *The Power of Bankruptcy Courts to Shift Fees under the Equal Access to Justice Act* 61 University of Chicago Law Review 985 (1994). Tort cases against the United *States* are brought under the Federal Tort Claims Act (FTCA 28 U.S.C. § 1346(b). 2671-2680. The FTCA requires that, prior to filing suit, a claimant must first present his claim to the federal agency out of whose activities his claim arose. If the claim is settled before suit is filed, the claimant's attorney may receive up to 20 percent of the settlement, if it is not, the claimant's attorney may receive up to 25 percent of a court award or settlement 28 U.S.C. § 2678 (See 86 ALR Fed 866. Fee awards against the United States by 28 U.S.C. § 2412 (b), In Sanchez v. *Rowe,* 870 F.2d 291, 295 (5th Cir. 1989), the court found a lack of the requisite bad faith and therefore did "not reach the issue whether an award of attorneys fees would... be barred by the FTCA prohibition against punitive damages [28 U.S.C. § 2674]." Subsequently, however, in *Molzof v. United States,* 502 U.S. 301, 312 (1992), the Supreme Court, in a different context, held "that § 2674 bars the recovery only of what are legally considered 'punitive damages' under traditional common-law principles." (Emphasis in original)

15 The EAJA does not specify which party has the burden of proof as to whether the position of the United States was substantially justified or special circumstances make an award unjust. However, the conference report to the original EAJA states: "After a prevailing party has submitted an application for an award, the burden of proving that a fee award should not be made rests with the Government." H.Rept. 96-1434, at 22, The "position" of the United States which the government must prove to have been substantially justified in order to avoid a fee award includes both the conduct of the government in the proceeding itself and the action of the government that gave rise to the proceeding. *5* U.S.C. § 504(b)(1)(E); 28 U.S.C. § 2412(d)(2)(D).

16 These limitations are incorporated into Public Law 105-119, which authorizes awards of attorneys' fees to prevailing criminal defendants, and is discussed at pp. *59-60, infra.*

17 The two exceptions are tax-exempt organizations and agricultural cooperatives; they may recover fees regardless of their net worth but apparently may not recover fees if they have more than 500 employees. *See,* 5 U.S.C. § 504(b)(l)(B); 28 U.S.C. § 2412(d)(2)(B); Unification Church v. Immigration & Naturalization Service, 762 F.2d 1077 (D.C. Cir. 1985).

> If, in a civil action brought by the United States or a proceeding for judicial review of an adversary adjudication described in section 504(a)(4) of title 5, the demand by the United States [other than a recitation of the maximum statutory penalty] is substantially in excess of the judgment finally obtained by the United States and is unreasonable when compared with such judgment, under the facts and circumstances of the case, the court shall award to the party the fees and other expenses related to defending against the excessive demand, unless the party has committed a willful violation of law or otherwise acted in bad faith, or special circumstances make an award unjust. Fees and expenses awarded under this paragraph shall be paid only as a consequence of appropriations provided in advance.

This provision thus authorizes fee awards in favor of *losing* parties and in that respect is unique in the law of attorneys' fees.

In *Pierce v. Underwood,* 487 U.S. 552 (1988), the Supreme Court decided three issues concerning EAJA: (1) the applicable standard of appellate review, (2) the meaning of "substantially justified," and (3) the "special factors" that allow a court to award more than $75 per hour.

(1) Standard of Review. *Pierce* v. *Underwood* addressed the standard that a federal court of applies in reviewing a decision of a federal district court under EAJA. Either party may appeal a district court's decision under EAJA, and, as the Supreme Court explained:

> For purposes of standard of review, decisions by judges are traditionally divided into three categories, denominated questions of law (reviewable *de novo),* questions of fact (reviewable for clear error), and matters of discretion (reviewable for "abuse of discretion").

487 U.S. at 558.

The Supreme Court found that EAJA did not provide a clear prescription as to the appropriate standard of review (unlike, for example, 42 U.S.C. § 1988(b), which provides that "the court, in its discretion, may allow the prevailing party... a reasonable attorney's fee"). The Court, therefore, for a variety of reasons, held that the "abuse of discretion" standard was most appropriate for appeals of EAJA court decisions.

Awards of attorneys' fees under EAJA at the agency level may be appealed to a court only by the prevailing party, not by the United States. The statute, at 5 U.S.C. § 504(c)(2*),* provides:

> The court's determination on any appeal heard under this paragraph shall be based solely on the factual record made before the agency. The court may modify the determination of fees and other expenses only if the court finds that the failure to

make an award of fees and other expenses, or the calculation of the amount of the award, was unsupported by substantial evidence.

Prior to the 1985 amendments to EAJA, this provision stated that the court could modify an agency decision only if it found "an abuse of discretion." It was intended that the new standard — "unsupported by substantial evidence" — permit "a broader scope of review...consistent with the normal scope of judicial review of agency actions."[18]

(2) "Substantially justified."[19] The United States may avoid liability for attorneys' fees under EAJA by proving that its position "was substantially justified or that special circumstances make an award unjust." 5 U.S.C. § 504(a)(l), 28 U.S.C. § 2412(d). The legislative history of the original EAJA stated that "[t]he test of whether the Government position is substantially justified is essentially one of reasonableness in law and fact."[20] Twelve of the thirteen federal circuits subsequently interpreted "substantially justified" to mean reasonable. *See, Pierce* v. *Underwood,* 487 U.S. at 565-566. The U.S. Court of Appeals for the District of Columbia was the exception. It reasoned:

> The Senate Judiciary Committee considered and rejected an amendment to the bill that would have changed the pertinent language from "substantially justified" to "reasonably justified." S.Rept. 253 [96th Cong., 1st Sess.] at 8. That refusal suggests that the test should, in fact, be slightly more stringent than "one of reasonableness."[21]

According to this view, the government's position maybe reasonable, yet fail to be substantially justified, making it easier to recover fees under the substantially justified standard than under a reasonableness standard. The 1985 amendments to BAJA did not alter the text of the substantially justified language, but an accompanying committee report expressed support for the D.C. Circuit's interpretation:

> Several courts have held correctly that "substantial justification" means more than merely reasonable. Because in 1980 Congress rejected a standard of "reasonably justified" in favor of "substantially justified," the test must be more than just reasonableness.[22]

---

18 H.Rept. 99-120, 99th Cong., 1st Sess. 16 (1985), *reprinted in* 1985 U.S.C.C.A.N. 132, 145.

19 Cases construing this term as used in the EAJA are collected at 69 ALR Fed 130.

20 H.Rept. 96-1434, 96th Cong., 2d Sess. 22 (1980), *reprinted* in 1980 U.S.C.C.A.N, 5003, 5011.

21 Spencer v. National Labor Relations Board, 712 F.2d 539, 558 (D.C. Cir. 1983), *cert. denied,* 466 U.S. 936 (1984).

22 H.Rept. 99-120, 99th Cong.. 1st Sess. 9(1985), *reprinted in* 1985 U.S.C.C.A.N. 132, 138.

The Supreme Court in *Pierce v. Underwood* held that substantially justified means reasonable. The Court found that a "more than mere reasonableness" test would be "out of accord with prior usage" and "unadministerable." "Between the test of reasonableness," the Court wrote, "and a test such as 'clearly and convincingly justified'... there is simply no accepted stopping-place, no ledge that can hold the anchor for steady and consistent judicial behavior." 487 U.S. at 568. The Court found that the 1985 committee report was not controlling because it was neither "(1) an authoritative interpretation of what the 1980 statute meant, or (2) an authoritative expression of what the 1985 Congress intended." *Id.* at 566.

(3) Exceeding $75 (now $125) per hour. EAJA provides that fees "shall be based upon prevailing market rates for the kind and quality of the services furnished," but "shall not be awarded in excess of $75 [$125 for cases commenced on or after March 29, 1996] per hour unless the court determines that an increase in the cost of living or a special factor, such as the limited availability of qualified attorneys for the proceedings involved, justifies a higher fee." 28 U.S.C. § 2412(d)(2)(A)(ii). (The same cap applies in agency proceedings; *see,* 5 U.S.C. § 504(b)(l)(A)). The Court in *Pierce v. Underwood* held:

> If "the limited availability of qualified attorneys for the proceedings involved" meant merely that lawyers skilled and experienced enough to try the case are in short supply, it would effectively eliminate the $75 cap — since the "prevailing market rates for the kind and quality of the services furnished" are obviously *determined* by the relative supply and quality of services.... We think it refers to attorneys having some distinctive knowledge or specialized skill needful for the litigation in question — as opposed to an extraordinary level of the general lawyerly knowledge and ability useful in all litigation. Examples of the former would be an identifiable practice specialty such as patent law, or knowledge of foreign law or language.

487 U.S. at 571-572.

As for other "special factors," the Court wrote:

> For the same reason of the need to preserve the intended effectiveness of the $75 cap, we think the other "special factors" envisioned by the exception must be such as are not of broad and general application. We need not specify what they might be... .

Id. at *573.*

The Court, however, specified some items which are *not* special factors for purposes of exceeding the $75 per hour cap: "the novelty and difficulty of issues," "the undesirability of the case," "the work and ability of counsel," "the results obtained," "customary fees and awards in other cases," and "the contingent nature of the fee." All these "are factors applicable to a broad spectrum of litigation; they are little more than routine reasons why market rates are what they are." *Id.*

In *Commissioner, Immigration, and Naturalization Service v. Jean,* 496 U.S. 154 (1990), the Supreme Court held that, under EAJA, a prevailing party may recover attorneys' fees for services rendered in seeking a fee award without regard to whether the position of the United States was substantially justified. If the prevailing party is entitled to fees in the main action, then he is automatically entitled to fees for the time spent seeking fees. To hold otherwise could "spawn a 'Kafkaesque judicial nightmare' of infinite litigation for the last round of litigation over fees." *Id.* at 163.[23]

THE DUAL STANDARD: PREVAILING PLAINTIFFS AND PREVAILING DEFENDANTS

Most federal fee-shifting provisions authorize courts to award fees if "the fee claimant was the 'prevailing party,' the substantially prevailing party,' or 'successful.'" *Ruckelshaus v. Sierra Club.* 463 U.S. 680, 684 (1983). Although most of these statutes on their face do not distinguish between prevailing plaintiffs and prevailing defendants, the Supreme Court has held that Congress intended that under the civil rights statutes a dual standard should be applied in determining the appropriateness of fee awards to prevailing plaintiffs and prevailing defendants.[24]

In *Newman v. Piggie Park Enterprises, Inc.,* 390 U.S. 400 (1968), the Court considered 42 U.S.C. § 2000a-3(b), the provision in Title II of the Civil Rights Act of 1964 that provides for discretionary fee awards to prevailing parties. Noting that a plaintiff who is successful in a Title II suit vindicates "a policy that Congress considered of the highest priority" — enjoining racial discrimination — the Court held that under Title II a successful plaintiff "should ordinarily recover an attorney's fee unless special circumstances would render an award unjust." *Id.* at 402.

In *Albemarle Paper Co. v. Moody,* 422 U.S. 405 (1975), the Court held that the *Piggie Park* standard of awarding attorneys' fees to a successful plaintiff is equally applicable under Title VII of the Civil Rights Act, 42 U.S.C. § 2000e-5(k).

In *Christiansburg Garment Co. v. Equal Employment Opportunity Commission,* 434 U.S. 412, 417 (1978), the Court was faced with the question "what standard should inform a district court's discretion in deciding whether to award attorney's fees

---

[23] Annotations concerning the EAJA include 69 ALR Fed 130, 96 ALR Fed. 275, 96 ALR Fed 336, 105 ALR Fed 110,106 ALR Fed 191,107 ALR Fed 827, and 113 ALR Fed 267.

[24] Cases that interpret an attorneys' fees provision of one civil fights statute generally apply to the attorneys' fees provisions of all civil rights statutes, as they are all generally modeled on the fee-shifting provisions of the Civil Rights Act of 1964. The Supreme Court has noted "that fee-shifting statutes' similar language is a 'strong indication' that they are to be interpreted alike." Independent Federation of Flight Attendants v. Zipes, 491 U.S. 754, 758 n.2 (1989).

to a successful *defendant* in a Title VII action?" The Court noted that the statute on its face provided "no indication whatever of the circumstances under which either a plaintiff *or* defendant should be entitled to attorney's fees," and found that there are "strong equitable considerations" counseling a dual standard in determining the appropriateness of fee awards in the two situations. *Id.* at 418. Although prevailing plaintiffs should ordinarily recover attorneys' fees unless special circumstances would render an award unjust, prevailing defendants should recover fees only upon a finding that a plaintiffs action was "frivolous, unreasonable, or without foundation," although a finding that the action was brought in subjective bad faith is not necessary. *Id.* at 421. (A finding of subjective bad faith entitles either prevailing plaintiffs or defendants to a fee award under the common law exception to the American rule.)

The reason for the dual standard "is that while Congress wanted to clear the way for suits to be brought under the Act, it also wanted to protect defendants from burdensome litigation having no legal or factual basis." *Id.* at 420. Awarding fees to prevailing plaintiffs in the ordinary case will encourage suits to vindicate the public interest, but awarding fees to defendants in the ordinary case might have a chilling effect on the institution of such Suits. Awarding fees to defendants in frivolous cases, however, may discourage such suits.[25]

In *Hughes v. Rowe,* 449 U.S. 5, 14 (1980), the Supreme Court discussed the applicability of the *Christiansburg* standard for awards of attorneys' fees to prevailing defendants under the Civil Rights Attorney's Fees Awards Act of 1976, 42 U.S.C. § 1988(b):

> Although arguably a different standard might be applied in a civil rights action under 42 U.S.C. § 1983, we can perceive no reason for applying a less stringent standard. The plaintiffs action must be meritless in the sense that it is groundless or without foundation. The fact that a plaintiff may ultimately lose his case is not in itself a sufficient justification for the assessment of fees.

With respect to awards under § 1988(b) to prevailing plaintiffs, the court of appeals in *Brown v. Culpepper,* 559 F.2d 274, 278 (5th Cir. 1977), wrote:

---

[25] In *Durrett v. Jenkins Brickvard, Inc.,* 678 F.2d 911(11th Cir. 1982), the court held that a Title VII plaintiff is not relieved from liability for attorneys' fees by the fact that his attorney was primarily responsible for the fact that his lawsuit was frivolous, unreasonable, or without foundation. The court wrote:

> In virtually all actions without legal basis, and in many without factual basis, it will be the plaintiffs attorney who should first recognize the insufficiency of the case... If plaintiffs in such cases were permitted to escape liability under § 706 [42 U.S.C. § 2000e-5(k)], the salutary effect of that provision would be diluted. ...[I]n many cases... in which the plaintiffs counsel may appear to be primarily culpable, the plaintiff may find relief from the effect of our rule in the form of malpractice action.

Id. at 916.

> In Title II and Title VII [of the Civil Rights Act of 1964] cases the Fifth Circuit has held that the defendant's conduct, be it negligent or intentional, in good faith or bad, is irrelevant to an award of attorneys' fees [citations omitted]. We now hold that, consistent with congressional intent, the same standard should apply to section 1988.

In *Independent Federation of Flight Attendants v. Zipes,* 491 U.S. 754,755,761 (1989), the Supreme Court held that, under Title VII of the Civil Rights Act of 1964, a court may "award attorney's fees against intervenors who have not been found to have violated the Civil Rights Act or any other federal law... only where the intervenors' action was frivolous, unreasonable, or without foundation."

The dual standard has also been held applicable to the attorneys' fees provisions in federal environmental statutes.[26] However, it apparently is "more difficult for an environmental plaintiff than a civil rights plaintiff to recover an attorney fee."[27]

The Supreme Court has held that the dual standard does not apply under the attorneys' fees provision of the Copyright Act, 17 U.S.C. § 505, which, like those of the civil rights statutes, does not distinguish on its face between plaintiffs and defendants. In *Fantasy, Inc. v. Fogerty,* 510 U.S. 717, 527 (1994), the Court held that, in contrast with the civil rights statutes, under the Copyright Act, "defendants who seek to advance a variety of meritorious copyright defenses should be encouraged to litigate them to the same extent that plaintiffs are encouraged to litigate meritorious claims of infringement." The Court rejected both the dual standard and "the British Rule for automatic recovery of attorney's fees by the prevailing party.

Prevailing plaintiffs and prevailing defendants are to be treated alike, but attorney's fees are to be awarded to prevailing parties only as a matter of the court's discretion." *Id.* at 534.

The Concept of Prevailing Party

The phrase "prevailing party" is not limited to a victor only after entry of a final judgment following a fill trial on the merits. "The fact that respondent prevailed through a settlement rather than through litigation does not weaken her claim to fees." *Maher v. Gagne,* 448 U.S. 122, 129 (1980). Permitting fee awards upon favorable settlements encourages prevailing parties to settle, thereby lessening docket congestion, and it prevents losing parties from escaping liability for fees merely by conceding cases before final judgment.

---

26 Consolidated Edison Co. v. Realty Investment Associates, 524 F. Supp. 150 (S.D.N.Y. 1981).

27 Mary Frances Derfner and Arthur D. Wolf, 1 COURT AWARDED ATTORNEY FEES, ¶ 8.02[2], pp. 8-9 (Matthew Bender, 1997) (attributing this fact to the Supreme Court's decision 111 *Ruckelshaus,* discussed below at p. 16).

The simplest means of providing for an award is through a stipulation in the settlement that a particular party has prevailed and that a specified amount constitutes reasonable attorneys' fees. It has been held that, in settled cases in which courts are called upon to determine entitlement to attorneys' fees, judges should engage in "a close scrutiny of the totality of circumstances surrounding the settlement, focusing particularly on the necessity for bringing the action and whether the party is the successful party with respect to the central issue." Use of this standard will prevent fee awards in "nuisance settlements."[28]

Plaintiffs may also be deemed prevailing for purposes of attorneys' fees when no judgment or settlement occurs, but their suit serves as a catalyst in prompting the defendant to alter his conduct. One court held that, to recover fees in these circumstances, plaintiffs must "establish causation between their litigation and 'some of the benefits' they sought."[29] However, another court said that the term "prevailing party" in Title VII of the Civil Rights Act of 1964 should not be "extended beyond a courtroom context to include actual effect on corporate policy."[30] In addition, in dictum in *Farrar v. Hobby,* 506 U.S. 103, 111 (1992), the Supreme Court said that to be a prevailing party under 42 U.S.C. § 1988(b), "[t]he plaintiff must obtain an enforceable judgment against the defendant from whom fees are sought... or comparable relief through a consent decree or settlement... ." However, the issue in this case was the extent to which a plaintiff who wins only nominal damages is entitled to a fee award, and the Court did not address the issue of plaintiffs who serve merely as catalysts.[31]

In cases that are litigated to conclusion, a party may be deemed to have prevailed for purposes of a fee award prior to the losing party's having exhausted its final appeal. However, a party that prevails at the trial level will ultimately be entitled to a fee award only if it finally prevails on appeal.[32] A party awarded fees upon prevailing at the trial level apparently may be precluded from collecting them pending appeal; Federal Rule of Civil Procedure 62 (28 U.S.C. App. Rule 62) provides for a stay of proceedings to enforce a judgment pending appeal. If a party that prevails at the trial

---

[28] Parker v. Matthews, 411 F. Supp. *1059,* 1064 (D.DC. 1976), *aff'd sub nom.* Parker v. Califano, 561 F.2d 320 (D.C. Cir, 1977).

[29] NAACP v. Wilmington Medical Center, Inc., 689 F.2d 1161, 1167 (3d Cir. 1983), *rehearing denied,* 693 F.2d 22 (3d Cir, 1983), *cert. denied,* 460 U.S. 1052 (1983).

[30] Williams v. General Foods Corp., 492 F.2d 399, 408 (7th Cir. 1974).

[31] The holding of *Farrar v. Hobby* is discussed at page 18, below. On the implications for the catalyst theory of the dictum quoted above, see, Joel H. Trotter, *The Catalyst Theory of Civil Rights Fee Shifting After* Farrar v. Hobby, 80 Virginia Law Review 1429 (1994).

[32] *See,* Poelker v. Doe, 432 U.S. 519, 521 n.2 (1977). Fee awards may include amounts incurred in litigation over the fee award. *See,* 16 ALR Fed 643, § 10, However, in *Jensen V. Guy of San Jose,* 806 F.2d 899 (9th Cir. 1986) (en banc), the defendant prevailed on the merits and was awarded fees. On appeal, the fee award (but not the decision on the merits) was overturned, and the plaintiff was held ineligible to recover attorneys' fees incurred in overturning the fee award.

level should collect a fee award and subsequently lose the case on appeal, it apparently would be obligated to return the money.

A party may also be deemed to have prevailed even before final disposition at the trial level. In *Bradley v. Richmond School Board,* 416 U.S. 696, 723 (1974), the Supreme Court wrote:

> To delay a fee award until the entire litigation is concluded would work a substantial hardship on plaintiffs and their counsel, and discourage the institution of actions.... A district court must have the discretion to award fees and costs incident to the final disposition of interim matters.

At what stage of the litigation may a party be entitled to an interim award? In *Bradley* the Court would:

> say only that the entry of any order that determines substantial rights of the parties may be an appropriate occasion upon which to consider the propriety of an award of counsel fees ....

Id. at 723 n.28.

In *Bradley,* the statute under which fees were awarded, 20 U.S.C. § 1617 (since repealed), permitted awards only "[u]pon entry of a final order by a court of the United States." The Court, in allowing an interim award under this statute, noted that "many final orders may issue in the course of litigation." *Id.* at 723. In the case of a statute or common law rule that permits fee awards to prevailing parties but does not expressly make entry of a final order a prerequisite for such awards, fee awards may be appropriate at some stage of the litigation prior to entry of an interim final order.

Some courts have required recipients of interim awards to post bonds to insure recovery of the awards and interest should the recipients ultimately lose.[33]

In *Hanrahan v. Hampton,* 446 U.S. 754 (1980), a district court had directed verdicts for the defendants, but the court of appeals had reversed and ordered a new trial. The court of appeals had also ordered the defendants, under the Civil Rights Attorney's Fees Awards Act of 1976, 42 U.S.C. § 1988(b), to pay the attorneys' fees incurred by the plaintiffs during the course of their appeal. The Supreme Court reversed the award of attorneys' fees on the ground that the plaintiffs were not "prevailing" parties as required by the statute as a condition for a fee award. The Court concluded that, under § 1988(b), although "a person may in some circumstances be a 'prevailing party' without having obtained a favorable 'final judgment following a full trial on the merits,'" a party must have "established his entitlement to some

---

[33] Nicodemus v. Chrysler Corp. — Toledo Machining Plant, 445 F. Supp. 559 (ND. Ohio 1977), *rev'd on other grounds,* 596 F.2d 152 (6th Cir. 1979); Howard v. Phelps, 443 F. Supp. 374 (ED. La. 1978).

relief on the merits of his claims, either in the trial court or on appeal." Being granted the right to a new trial was not a victory on the merits; nor were any favorable procedural or evidentiary rulings victories on the merits, even though they may affect the disposition on the merits.[34]

In *Hewitt v. Helms,* 482 U.S. 755 (1987), the Supreme Court held that, under § 1988(b), a plaintiff was not entitled to a fee award where "[t]he most that he obtained was an interlocutory ruling [by a court of appeals] that his complaint should not have been dismissed for failure to state a constitutional claim." The court of appeals had "explicitly left it to the District Court 'to determine the appropriateness and availability of the requested relief,' *655* F.2d, at 503; the Court of Appeals granted no relief of its own, declaratory or otherwise." *Id.* at 760.

In *Rhodes v. Stewart,* 488 U.S. 1,4(1988) (per curiam), the Supreme Court held that a declaratory judgment, like any other judgment, "will constitute relief, for purposes of § 1988(b), if, and only if, it affects the behavior of the defendant towards the plaintiff. In this case, there was no such result." In this case, two prisoners had sued prison officials for refusing to allow them to subscribe to a magazine. They won declaratory relief, but only after one had died and the other had been released from prison.

In *Ruckelshaus v. Sierra Club,* 463 u.s 680. 694 (1983). the Supreme Court held that § 307(f) of the Clean Air Act, 42 U.S.C. § 7607(f). authorizes awards of attorneys' fees only to plaintiffs who have "some degree of success on the merits." This statute, as well as other federal environmental laws, provides: "In any judicial proceeding under this section, the court may award costs of litigation (including reasonable attorney and expert witness fees) whenever it determines that such an award is appropriate." On their face, these statutes allow fee awards even to parties who do not prevail, and, in the case under consideration, the court of appeals had awarded fees to such a party, holding that it was "appropriate" for it to receive fees for its contributions to the goals of the Clean Air Act.

The Supreme Court acknowledged that the legislative history of the Act stated that it was not intended that fee awards "should be restricted to cases in which the party seeking fees was the 'prevailing party." 463 U.S. at 687. The Court noted, however, that, prior to enactment of § 307(f), some courts had interpreted the phrase "prevailing party" in various fee-shifting statutes as limited to a party who prevailed "essentially" on "central issues." *Id.* at 688. When Congress said that awards under §

---

[34] The Court's holding in *Hanrahan* apparently applies to cases brought under Title II and Title VII of the Civil Rights Act of 1964, 42 U. S.C. §§ 2000a-3(b) and 2000e-5(k), and § 402 of the Voting Rights Act Amendments of 1975, 42 U.S.C. § 19731(e), because, as the Court noted, § 1988(b) was patterned on these statutes. 446 U.S. at 758 n.4. Under Title VII, a party who prevails on an interlocutory appeal apparently is entitled to attorneys' fees at least "when an interlocutory appeal results in a final resolution of a separable dispute." Grubbs v. Butz, 548 F.2d 973, 975 n.5 (D.C. Cir. 1976). *See also,* Smith v. University of North Carolina, 632 F.2d 316 (4fh Cir. 1980);Van Hoomissen v. Xerox Corp., 503 F.2d 1131 (9th Cir. 1974).

307(f) should not be restricted to prevailing parties, it meant, the Court held, merely to eliminate these restrictive readings of the phrase "prevailing party." Specifically, Congress meant only "to expand the class of parties eligible for fee awards from prevailing parties to *partially prevailing parties* — parties achieving *some success,* even if not major success" (emphasis supplied by Court). *Id.*[35]

In *Hensley v. Eckerhart,* 461 U.S. 424, 433 (1983), the Supreme Court noted that "plaintiffs may be considered 'prevailing parties' for attorney's fees purposes if they succeed on any significant issue in litigation which achieves some of the benefit the parties sought in bringing suit." However, if the plaintiffs achieve only *some* of the benefit, then they will not necessarily be entitled to a full award of attorneys' fees. The Court addressed the issue of whether, under 42 U.S.C. § 1988(b), "a partially prevailing plaintiff may recover an attorney's fee for legal services on unsuccessful claims." *Id.* at 426. The Court held:

> Where the plaintiff has failed to prevail on a claim that is distinct in all respects from his successful claims, the hours spent on the unsuccessful claim should be excluded in considering the amount of a reasonable fee. Where a lawsuit consists of related claims, a plaintiff who has won substantial relief should not have his attorney's fee reduced simply because the district court did not adopt each contention raised. But where the plaintiff achieved only limited success, the district court should award only that amount of fees that is reasonable in relation to the results obtained.

Id. At 440.

As for how to determine the amount of fees that is reasonable when the plaintiff achieves only limited success, the Court wrote:

> There is no precise rule or formula for making these determinations. The district court may attempt to identify specific hours that should be eliminated, or it may simply reduce the award to account for the limited success. The court necessarily has discretion in making this equitable judgment.

Id. at 43 6-437.

---

35 1996, the Equal Access to Justice Act was amended to authorize fees to losing parties in some instances; *see,* page 8, *supra.* In footnote 1 of its opinion *Ruckelshaus,* the Court wrote:

> "Sixteen federal statutes and § 304(d) of the Clear Air Act contain provisions for awards of attorney's fees identical to § 307(f)." It then listed 13 of them. The others are the Solid Waste Disposal Act, 42 U.S.C. § 6792(e), and two sections of the Toxic Substances Control Act (TOSCA), 15 U.S.C. §§ 2619(c)(2) and 2620(b)(4)(C). (The Court did list a third section of TOSCA, 15 U.S.C. § 2618(d)). The Court then wrote: "As explained below [it did not explain below], the interpretation of 'appropriate' in § 307(f) controls construction of the term in these statutes." The interpretation of these other statutes had not been at issue in the case.

In *Texas State Teachers Association v. Garland Independent School District,* 489 U.S. 782 (1989), the Supreme Court held that, under 42 U.S.C. § 1988(b), although a party must prevail on a "significant" issue in order to be eligible for a fee award, it need not prevail on the "central" issue in the litigation. "[T]he *degree* of the plaintiffs success in relation to the other goals of the lawsuit is a factor critical to the determination of the size of a reasonable fee, not to eligibility for a fee award at all." *Id.* at 790 (emphasis in original).

In *Farrar v. Hobby,* 506 U.S. 103 (1992), the Supreme Court held that, under 42 U.S.C. § 1988(b), a plaintiff who is awarded only nominal damages—in this case one dollar when he had sought $17 million — is a prevailing party for attorneys' fees purposes. Nevertheless, "[w]hen a plaintiff recovers only nominal damages because of his failure to prove an essential element of his claim for monetary relief... , the only reasonable fee is usually no fee at all." *Id.* at 115. In this case, the plaintiff had established "the violation of his right to procedural due process but cannot prove actual injury." *Id.* at 112. Consequently, although he was a "prevailing party," he was entitled to no award of attorneys' fees.

Can a person receive an award of attorneys' fees for representing himself? In *Kay v. Ehrler,* 499 U.S. 432, 435 (1991), the Supreme Court noted that there is no disagreement "that a *pro se* litigant who is *not* a lawyer is *not* entitled to attorney's fees" under 42 U.S.C. § 1988(b). The question before the Court however was whether a *pro se* litigant who *is* an attorney is entitled to fees under § 1988(b). The Court found no answer in the statute or in its legislative history. It ruled against the attorney in an effort to create an incentive for attorneys not to represent themselves, because an attorney who represents himself "is deprived of the judgment of an independent third party." *Id.* at 437. It concluded that its decision would serve "[t]he statutory policy of furthering the successful prosecution of meritorious claims." *Id.* at 438. *Kay v. Ehrler* has been applied to other fee-shifting statutes, including the Equal Access to Justice Act, the Freedom of Information Act, the individuals with Disabilities Education Act, the Fair Debt Collection Practices Act, and Title VII of the Civil Rights Act of 1964.[36]

AWARDS OF ATTORNEYS' FEES INCURRED IN ADMINISTRATIVE PROCEEDINGS

Title VII of the Civil Rights Act of 1964, 42 U.S.C § 2000e-5(k), provides, in pertinent part:

---

36 Gregory Paul Barbee, *Attorney's Fee Awards to Pro Se Litigants After* Kay v. Ehrler: *No Fees. It's Simple. But is it Absolute?,* 69 Southern California Law Review 1795, 1817 (1996).

> In any action or proceeding under this subchapter the court, in its discretion, may allow the prevailing party… a reasonable attorney's fee as part of the costs.

In *New York Gaslight Club v. Carey,* 447 U.S. 54 (1980), the plaintiff sought relief for an alleged violation of Title VII of the Civil Rights Act of 1964, and filed a state administrative proceeding, as required by the Act, and a federal court suit. She won the state proceeding and agreed to a dismissal of the federal court suit, except for her request for attorneys' fees. The Supreme Court upheld her right to an award by the court of attorneys' fees incurred at the administrative level. The Court noted "Congress's use of the broadly inclusive disjunctive phrase 'action or proceeding'" (*id.* at 61) and added that it found nothing to indicate that "proceeding" was intended to apply only to federal agency proceedings. In dicta, the Court added that, for purposes of a fee award, it did not matter whether the plaintiff had lost at the administrative level and prevailed in court on the merits, or had prevailed at the administrative level and sued in court solely to recover attorneys' fees incurred at the administrative level. The Court wrote:

> It would be anomalous to award fees to the complainant who is unsuccessful or only partially successful in obtaining state or local remedies, but to deny an award to the complainant who is successful in fulfilling Congress' plan that federal policies be vindicated at the state or local level.

Id at 66.

Title VII's attorneys' fees provision has been a model for others. One of the statutes modeled on it was the Civil Rights Attorney's Fees Awards Act of 1976, 42 U.S.C § 1988(b). It provides:

> …or proceeding to enforce a … of sections 1981, 1981a, 1982, 1983, 1985 and 1986 of this title, title IX of Public Law 92-318, the Religious Freedom Restoration Act of 1993, title VI of the Civil Rights Act of 1964, or section 40302 of the Violence Against Women Act of 1994, the court, in its discretion may allow the prevailing party, other than the United States, a reasonable attorney's fee as part of the costs.

In *Webb v. County Board of Education of Dyer County, Tennessee,* 471 U.S. 234 (1985), the plaintiff lost an administrative hearing authorized by state law but subsequently prevailed in a federal court suit under 42 U.S.C. § 1983. He then filed a motion for an award under § 1988(b) of attorneys' fees incurred in both the hearing and the suit. The Supreme Court faced the same question it had in faced in *Gaslight* — the recoverability of fees incurred at the administrative level — but this time with respect to fee awards under 42 U.S.C. § 1988(b) in cases brought under 42 U.S.C. § 1983. Even though § 1988(b) contains the same "action or proceeding" language as Title VII, the Court held that § 1988(b) does not authorize awards of fees in § 1983 administrative proceedings. The basis for the different results in *Gaslight* and *Webb* was that under Title VII administrative proceedings are mandatory, but under § 1983 they are not, and it is only mandatory proceedings that are brought to "enforce" a federal civil rights statute. Because the plaintiff could have gone "straight to court to assert" his § 1983 claim, the Court found that:

> the school board proceedings in this case simply do not have the same integral function under § 1983 that state administrative proceedings have under Title VII.... Administrative proceedings... created by state law simply are not any part of the proceedings to enforce § 1983.

471 U.S. at 241.

The Court did not explicitly address whether the word "proceeding" in § 1988(b) had any reference in the context of a § 1983 "action or proceeding," but it did allow that attorneys' fees incurred in an administrative proceeding could be awarded in a § 1983 action to the extent "that any discrete portion of the work product from the administrative proceeding was work that was both useful and of a type ordinarily necessary to advance the civil rights litigation... ." *Id.* at 242.

The most recent Supreme Court decision to address the issue of awards of attorneys' fees incurred at the administrative level was *North Carolina Department of Transportation v. Crest Street Community Council, Inc.*, 479 U.S. 6 (1986). The plaintiffs in this case had prevailed in a federal administrative proceeding under Title VI of the Civil Rights Act of 1964, and sought to recover fees under § 1988(b) in an independent action in federal court. It might have been expected that the Supreme Court would decide whether § 1988(b) authorized an award of attorneys' fees incurred at the administrative level on the basis of whether an administrative proceeding under Title VI was mandatory, and therefore was a proceeding to enforce Title VI. However, the Court did not reach this issue because it rejected a fee award on a different ground: that an action solely to recover a fee award is not an action to enforce Title VI. The Court wrote:

> The plain language of § 1988 suggests the answer to the question of whether attorney's fees may be awarded in an independent action which is not to enforce any of the civil rights laws listed in § 1988. The section states that *in the action or proceeding to enforce* the civil rights laws listed—42 U.S.C. §§ 1981, 1982, 1983, 1985, 1986, Title IX, or Title VI — *the court* may award attorney's fees. The case before us is not, and was never, an action to enforce any of these laws. On its face, § 1988 does not authorize a court to award attorney's fees except in an action to enforce the listed civil rights laws. The legislative history of § 1988 supports the plain import of the statutory language.

Id. at 12.

This means that, under all the statutes listed in § 1988(b), a party who prevails at the administrative level may not bring a court action solely to recover a fee award. A party who loses an administrative proceeding, however, and prevails on the merits in court, may recover attorneys' fees incurred at both the administrative and court levels. He may recover fees incurred in an administrative proceeding in either of two situations: if the proceeding was one to enforce the statute *(i.e.,* was mandatory, or if *a* "discrete portion of the work product from the administrative proceedings... was both useful and of a type ordinarily necessary to advance the civil rights litigation...." *Id.* at 15, quoting *Webb,* 471 U.S. at 243.

The Court in *Crest Street* acknowledged that in *Gaslight* it had said that it would be "anomalous" to distinguish in this way between a party who sues in court solely to recover fees (after having prevailed at the administrative level) and one who sues also on the merits. In *Crest Street,* however, the Court referred to this comment in *Gaslight* as "dicta" *(id.* at 13), presumably because the plaintiff in *Gaslight* had filed a court action not solely to recover fees. The Court in *Crest Street* added:

> Moreover, we now believe that the paradoxical nature of this result may have been exaggerated. There are many types of behavior that may lead others to comply with civil rights laws. For example, an employee, after talking to his lawyer, may choose to discuss hiring or promotion practices with an employer, and as a result of this discussion the employer may alter those practices to comply more fully with employment discrimination laws. In some sense it may be considered anomalous that this employee's initiative would not be awarded with attorney's fees. But an award of attorney's fees under § 1988 depends not only on the results obtained, but also on what actions were needed to achieve those results. It is entirely reasonable to limit the award of attorney's fees to those parties who, in order to obtain relief, found it necessary to file a complaint in court.

Id. at 14.

The dissent in *Crest Street,* apart from disagreeing with the majority's interpretation of the language and the legislative history of § 1988(b), argued that the effect of the decision would be to burden federal courts by causing parties who are not required to exhaust administrative remedies to "immediately file suit in federal court to protect any possible claim for attorney's fees should they subsequently prevail." *Id.* at 21. In *Gaslight,* in fact, the Court had acknowledged "that if fees were authorized only when the complainant found an independent reason for suing in federal court under Title VII, such a ground almost always could be found." 447 U.S. at 66 n.6. Thus, *Crest Street* may have little practical import for Title VII.

It may also be argued that the reasoning of *Crest Street* does not even apply to Title VII. Although § 1988(b) was modeled on the attorneys fees provision of Title VII, there is a difference in their language that may be relevant. Section 1988(b) provides that a court may award attorneys' fees in any action or proceeding "to enforce" various civil rights statutes. Title VII, by contrast, says that a court may award fees in any action or proceeding "under this title" (as enacted) or "under this subchapter" (as codified), in either case referring to Title VII itself. Arguably, a suit solely to recover fees incurred in an administrative proceeding under Title VII is an action or proceeding *under* Title VII, even though a suit solely to recover fees incurred in an administrative proceeding under Title VI is not an action or proceeding *to enforce* Title VI. However, this may be an overly literal reading in that when the attorneys' fees provision in Title VII refers to an action or proceeding "under" Title VII, it may not have been intended that it refer to itself, but rather only to the rest of Title VII.[37]

The Supreme Court, in *Gaslight,* of course, has already interpreted this language and concluded that it "encompasses a suit solely to obtain an award of attorney's fees for legal work done in state and local proceedings." Yet in *Crest Street* the Court labeled as "dicta" its statement in *Gaslight* that to hold otherwise would be anomalous. It appears uncertain whether the Court would reach the result it reached in *Gaslight* in a Title VII case in which a court action was never filed on the merits.[38]

AWARDS OF ATTORNEYS' FEES BY ADMINISTRATIVE AGENCIES

An issue that has never reached the Supreme Court is whether administrative agencies themselves may award attorneys' fees under any of the civil rights statutes. Title VII's attorneys' fees provision and the statutes modeled on it authorize only "the court" to award fees, but, to the extent that a court may award fees incurred at the agency level, the question has arisen whether an agency itself may do so in order to save the parties and a federal court from litigation solely on a fee claim.[39] Of course,

---

37 In *Slade for Estate of Slade v. U.S. Postal Service,* 952 F.2d 357, 361 (10th Cir. 1991), the court wrote:

> Here, Plaintiffs claim for attorney's fees was brought pursuant to § 2000e-5(k), which provides for attorney's fees to the prevailing party "[i]n any action or proceeding under this subchapter [2000e]." The applicable statute here does not require that the federal court proceeding be brought to enforce [emphasis supplied by the court] the laws set forth in § 2000e. Therefore, Crest Street is not dispositive of the issue of jurisdiction in this case. (By "jurisdiction," the court meant subject matter jurisdiction to hear a claim solely for attorneys' fees.)

38 In *Jones v. American State Bank,* 857 F.2d 494 (8th Cir. 1988), the court of appeals affirmed a fee award under Title VII in a suit brought solely to recover fees incurred in a state administrative proceeding.

39 In a situation in which a party who prevails at the agency level may bring a court action solely to recover fees, the litigating arm of the agency of course may agree to a settlement with respect to a fee award, thereby avoiding litigation of the issue and the incurring of additional fees. The question raised

only if a court may award fees incurred at the administrative level will the question arise whether the agency itself may award such fees. There are two circumstances in which a court clearly may not award fees incurred at the administrative level: the circumstances of *Crest Street* and of *Webb.*

Crest Street prohibits courts from awarding fees in suits solely to recover fees, at least in suits under § 1988(b), so it seems clear that agencies may not award fees under § 1988. Assuming that the reasoning of *Crest Street* does not apply to some statutes, such as Title VII, *Webb* still would preclude courts from awarding fees incurred in non-mandatory administrative proceedings under such statutes, except to the extent that such fees cover "any discrete portion of the work product... that was both useful and of a type ordinarily necessary to advance the civil rights litigation." However, Title VII provides for mandatory administrative proceedings, so the question arises under Title VII whether an agency itself may award fees and thereby save the prevailing party from going to court.

The court of appeals in *Crest Street* had held that a party who prevailed in an administrative proceeding under Title VI could bring a court action under § 1988(b) solely to recover fees. The court of appeals in *Crest Street,* in addition, citing the fact that § 1988(b) on its face authorizes only "the court" to award fees, said in dicta that "it follows that plaintiffs *must* apply to a court for their fees." 769 F.2d at 1033 (emphasis in original). However, in *Smith v. Califano,* 446 F. Supp. 530 (D.D.C. 1978), the court held that an agency could award fees in a Title VII proceeding. It wrote:

> Title VII is a statute in which Congress already has specifically provided for an award of attorneys' fees. Although the expression of that exception [to the American Rule] is contained in the remedial authority of the courts, the rights protected by the courts are the very same fights the agencies are to protect. Thus, finding authority for the agency also to award counsel fees to one who prevails at the administrative level would not create a "far-reaching" exception to the Rule. Rather, it would make the existing exception applicable regardless of the stage at which that federal fight is protected.

Id. at 532-533.

In addition, the court noted:

> [A]lthough Title VII does not expressly state that an agency may award attorneys' fees, it does state that [in proceedings brought by federal employees] the agency is to enforce the Act "through appropriate remedies... as will effectuate the policies of this section..." 42 U.S.C. § 2000e-16(b) (Supp. V 1975). Because the "make-whole"

here is whether the adjudicating arm of the agency may award fees over the objections of the litigating arm.

> concept is one of those policies, this provision can be read to permit the agency to award attorneys' fees, thereby making whole one who appears before it.

Id at 533.

This decision was followed in two other Title VII cases.[40] However, two other cases in the same district came to the contrary conclusion, holding that a party who prevails at the agency level under Title VII must go to court to recover his fees.[41] In 1980, the EEOC issued a regulation (amended in 1987) providing that it or other federal agencies may award attorneys' fees to federal employees under Title VII. 29 C.F.R. § 1613.271(d). No reported case appears to have challenged the EEOC's authority to promulgate this regulation.

An argument may be made, however, that, if the reasoning of *Crest Street* applies to Title VII, then the legality of these regulations would be placed in doubt. For, if the reasoning of *Crest Street* applies, which means that courts may not award attorneys' fees incurred by parties who prevail at the administrative level, then the only basis for an agency to award fees would be the "appropriate remedies" provision. It is not clear, however, that *Smith v. Califano* would have reached the same result in the absence of the statute's authorizing courts to award fees. If, under *Crest Street,* courts cannot award fees to parties who prevail in administrative proceedings under Title VII, then to allow agencies to award fees apparently would constitute a "far-reaching" exception to the American rule. Before an agency may order a litigant to bear his adversary's expenses, "it must be granted clear statutory power by Congress."[42] The power to employ "appropriate remedies" might not be sufficient.

Two lower court cases have addressed the question of the recoverability of fees in administrative proceedings under the Rehabilitation Act. In *Department of Education v. Katherine D.,* 531 F. Supp. 517, 531 (D. Hawaii 1982), *rev'd on other grounds,* 727 F.2d 809 (9th Cir. 1983), *cert. denied,* 471 U.S. 1117 (1985), the district court held that it could award attorneys' fees for services rendered in connection with both judicial and administrative proceedings under § 504 of the Act. In *Watson v. United States Veterans Administration,* 88 F.R.D. 267 (C.D. Cal. 1980), a district court held that the agency itself could award fees under § 501 of the Act. The court, citing *Smith v. Califano,* held that construing § 501 "to authorize the agency to award attorney's fees is more in keeping with the purpose of the statute and the intent of Congress than the contrary interpretation." 88 F.R.D. at 269. The court noted that the "'appropriate remedies' concept" is "incorporated in the Rehabilitation Act from Title VII." *Id.* at

---

40 Patton v. Andrus, 459 F. Supp. 1189 (D.D.C. 1978); and Williams v. Boorstin, 451 F. Supp. 1117 (D.D.C, 1978), *rev'd on other grounds,* 663 F.2d 109 (D.C. Cir, 1980), *cert. denied,* 451 U.S. 985 (1981).

41 Noble v. Claytor, 448 F. Supp. 1242 (D.D.C. 1978); Taylor v. Claytor, 15 EPD § 7854 (D.D.C. 1977).

42 Turner v. Federal Communications Commission, 514 F.2d 1354 (D.C. Cir. 1975).

268.[43] Notwithstanding this decision, if the reasoning of *Crest Street* precludes courts from awarding fees in suits solely to recover attorneys' fees incurred in administrative proceedings under the Rehabilitation Act. then it apparently would also preclude agencies from awarding fees. However. in 1987 the EEOC amended the regulation cited above (29 C.F.R. § 1613.271(d)) to authorize federal agencies to award attorneys' fees in proceedings under § 501 or § 505 of the Rehabilitation Act.

Awards of Attorneys' Fees in Civil Rights Cases

All federal civil rights laws permit awards of attorneys' fees and the major litigation concerning fee awards has occurred under these laws. Some aspects of these laws have already been discussed: the dual standard they have been construed to include, the meaning of the term "prevailing" they contain, and the extent to which they permit awards of fees incurred in administrative proceedings. This section of the report quotes or summarizes each attorney's fee provision applicable to a civil rights law, and discusses significant court decisions not covered in the discussions of the aspects of these laws just mentioned.

Civil Rights Act of 1964, Title II — Public Accommodations

Title II prohibits discrimination and segregation on the basis of race, color, religion, or national origin in places of public accommodation such as hotels, restaurants, gasoline stations, theaters, and other places of exhibition or entertainment, if their operations affect commerce or if their acts of discrimination or segregation are supported by state action. 42 U.S.C. § 2000a. Title II's attorneys' fees provision, 42 U.S.C. § 2000a-3(b), states:

> the court, in its discretion, may allow the prevailing party, other than the United States, a reasonable attorney's fee as part of the costs, and the United States shall be liable for costs the same as a private person.[44]

In addition, the court may appoint an attorney for a complainant. 42 U.S.C. § 2000a-3(a).

---

43 The concept is mentioned in § 505(a)(1), 29 U.S.C § 794a(1), which makes available to persons aggrieved by a violation of § 501 "[t]he remedies, procedures, and rights set forth in" Title VII.

44 Cases under this provision are collected at 16 ALR Fed 621.

Civil Rights Act of 1964, Title III — Public Facilities

Title III gives the Attorney General the authority to bring a civil action on behalf of any person unable to initiate and maintain appropriate legal proceedings who claims:

> that he is being deprived of or threatened with the loss of his right to equal protection of the laws, on account of his race, color, religion, or national origin, by being denied equal utilization of any public facility which is owned, operated, or managed by or on behalf of any State or subdivision thereof other than a public school or public college, as defined in section 2ilOilc of this title

42 U.S.C. § 2000b(a).

In any action under Title III "the United States shall be liable for costs, including reasonable attorney's fee, the same as a private person." 42 U.S.C. § 2000b-1.

Civil Rights Act of 1964, Title VII — Equal Employment Opportunities

Title VII prohibits discrimination by employers, employment agencies, and labor organizations on the basis of race, color, religion, sex, or national origin. Before an individual may bring a civil action in federal court under Title VII, he must file a charge with the Equal Employment Opportunity Commission (EEOC), which will attempt to resolve the complaint.[45] However, if the individual alleges discrimination in a state or locality that prohibits it, then federal proceedings must be deferred until relief through state or local proceedings has been sought. 42 U.S.C. § 2000e-5(c). If the matter does end up in federal court, the court may appoint an attorney for the complainant. 42 U.S.C. § 2000e-5(f)(1). Relief may include injunctions and "such affirmative action as may be appropriate, which may include, but is not limited to, reinstatement or hiring of employees, with or without back pay...." 42 U.S.C. §2000e-5(g)."[46]

Title VII's attorneys' fees provision, 42 U.S.C. § 2000e-5(k), provides:

---

[45] Prior to 1979, federal employees filed discrimination charges with the Civil Service Commission (CSC). Pursuant Reorganization Plan No. 1 of 1978, the function of the CSC in this regard was transferred to the EEOC by Executive Order 12106 (44 Fed. Reg. 1053 (Jan. 3, 1979)). (Reorganization Plan No. 2 of 1978 abolished the CSC.)

[46] Title VII has been held not to include compensatory damages; consequently, a teacher who retired before bringing suit based on discriminatory working conditions could not be a "prevailing party" eligible to recover attorneys' fees, although she had proved discrimination. Harrington v. Vandalia-Butler Board of Education, 585 F.2d 192 (6th Cir. 1978).

> In any action or proceeding under this subchapter the court, in its discretion, may allow the prevailing party, other than the Commission or the United States, a reasonable attorney's fee (including expert fees) as part of the costs, and the Commission and the United States shall be liable for costs the same as a private person.[47]

Title VII's attorneys' fees provision on its face bars awards in favor of the EEOC or the United States. In 1964, when the provision was enacted, Title VII did not apply to federal workers, so the United States at the time could be only a plaintiff in a Title VII suit. The 1972 amendments that made it possible for the United States to be a defendant under the Act did not amend the attorneys' fees provision, and, in *Copeland v. Martinez,* 603 F.2d 981 (D.C. Cir. 1979), *cert, denied,* 444 U.S. 1044 (1980), the issue arose whether an employee who sues the United States maybe held liable for attorneys' fees. In this case the employee was found to have sued in bad faith, so the court did not have to decide whether Title VII affirmatively authorizes fee awards to the federal government as defendant. The court held only "that § 706(k) does not preclude a court from awarding the United States its attorneys' fees [under the common law exception] when it has been sued in bad faith." *Id.* at 987.

Of course, as discussed above, even if the United States is entitled to fees as a prevailing defendant under Title VII in the absence of bad faith on the part of the plaintiff, it may recover only upon a finding that the plaintiffs suit was "frivolous, unreasonable, or without foundation." Prevailing plaintiffs (other than the United States), in contrast, may recover fees "in all but very unusual circumstances." *Albemarle Paper Co. v. Moody,* 422 U.S. 405, 415 (1975).

Courts have held that in Title VII suits attorneys' fees may be awarded against state governments *(Fitzpatrick v. Bitzer,* 427 U.S. 445, 456 (1976)), and in favor of state governments *(Kutska v. California State College,* 564 F.2d 108 (3d Cir. 1977)).

Fair Housing Act

The Fair Housing Act, Title VIII of the Civil Rights Act of 1968, as amended by the Fair Housing Amendments Act of 1988, Public Law 100-430, prohibits discrimination on the basis of race, color, religion, sex, handicap, familial status (having children), or national origin in the sale or rental of housing, the financing of housing, or the provision of brokerage services. 42 U.S.C. §§ 3404-3606. An aggrieved person may bring a civil action, in which the prevailing party, other than the United States, may recover reasonable attorneys' fees and costs, with the United States liable for such fees and costs to the same extent as a private person. 42 U.S.C. §

[47] Cases under this provision are collected at 16 ALR Fed 643 and 77 ALR Fed 272.

3613(c).[48] Presumably, the dual standard that applies to the fee-shifting provisions of other federal civil rights statutes will apply here. The court may appoint an attorney for the plaintiff 42 U.S.C. § 3613(b).

In addition, the Secretary of Housing and Urban Development may bring an administrative proceeding, and the Attorney General may bring a civil action, against a violator. In either case, the prevailing party, other than the United States, may recover a reasonable attorney's fee and costs, except that the United States shall be liable for fees and costs only to the extent provided by the Equal Access to Justice Act. 42 U.S.C. §§ 3612(p), 3614(d).

Fair Labor Standards Act

The Fair Labor Standards Act, among other things, prohibits employers from discriminating on the basis of sex in the amount of wages paid employees for equal work, and it prohibits labor organizations from causing employers to so discriminate. 29 U.S.C. § 206(d). Section 216(b) of Title 29 provides that in actions to enforce such provision, the court:

> shall, in addition to any judgment awarded to the plaintiff or plaintiffs, allow a reasonable attorney's fee to be paid by the defendant, and costs of the action.

Age Discrimination in Employment Act of 1967

The Age Discrimination in Employment Act of 1967 (ADEA), 29 U.S.C. §§ 621 *et seq*., prohibits, with certain exceptions, employers, employment agencies, and labor organizations from discriminating on the basis of age against individuals who are at least 40 years old. Section 7(b) of the Act, 29 U.S.C. § 626(b), incorporates the attorneys' fees provision of the Fair Labor Standards Act, 29 U.S.C. § 216(b).[49]

In 1974, a section was added to the ADEA to protect federal employees from age discrimination. 29 U.S.C. § 633a. However, this section provides that other provisions of the ADEA shall not apply in the case of federal employees (29 U.S.C. § 633a(f)), and the section makes no reference to attorneys' fees. Consequently, it is unsettled whether they may be awarded to federal employees who prevail at the administrative or the judicial level.[50]

---

48 Cases under this provision are collected at 38 ALR Fed 164.

49 *See,* 24 ALR Fed 808, 862 on this point; *see,* 99 ALR Fed 30 on fee awards under the ADEA generally.

50 *See, e.g.,* Lewis v. Federal Prison Industries, Inc., 953 F.2d 1277 (11th Cir. 1992); Palmer v. General Services Administration, 787 F.2d 300 (8th Cir. 1986).

The Civil Service Reform Act of 1978 provides for awards of attorneys' fees "in accordance with the standards prescribed under § 706(k) of the Civil Rights Act of 1964 (42 U.S.C. 2000e(k)" to a federal "employee or applicant for employment" who is discriminated against "on the basis of age, as prohibited under §§ 12 and 15 of the Age Discrimination in Employment Act of 1976 (29 U.S.C. 631, 633a)." 5 U.S.C. §§ 7701(g)(2), 2302(b)(1)(B). However, these provisions of the Civil Service Reform Act authorize only the Merit Systems Protection Board (MSPB), not the EEOC, to award attorneys' fees, and federal employees who wish to file age discrimination complaints at the administrative level ordinarily must do so before the EEOC. The MSPB becomes involved in age discrimination complaints when it hears appeals of "mixed case" complaints, which are discrimination complaints that an employee or job applicant raises as an affirmative defense to an adverse action. 29 C.F.R.§ 1613.402.

Equal Credit Opportunity Act

The Equal Credit Opportunity Act, 15 U.S.C. §§ 1691 *et seq.,* makes it unlawful for any person, business, or governmental agency that regularly extends credit to discriminate against any credit applicant:

> (1) on the basis of race, color, religion, national origin, sex or marital status, or age (provided the applicant has the capacity to contract); (2) because all or part of the applicant's income derives from any public assistance program; or (3) because the applicant has in good faith exercised any right under the Consumer Credit Protection Act.

Section 1691e(d) provides that in any successful action to enforce the Act, "the costs of the action, together with a reasonable attorney's fee as determined by the court, shall be added to any damages awarded...."

Voting Rights Act of 1965

The Voting Rights Act's attorneys' fees provision, 42 U.S.C. § 1973*l*(e), provides:

> In any action or proceeding to enforce the voting guarantee of the fourteenth or fifteenth amendment, the court, in its discretion, may allow the prevailing party, other than the United States, a reasonable attorney's fee as part of the costs.[51]

---

[51] Cases under this provision are collected at 68 ALR Fed 206.

The Voting Accessibility for the Elderly and Handicapped Act, 42 U.S.C. § 1973ee-4(c), provides:

> Notwithstanding any other provision of law, no award of attorney fees may be made with respect to an action under this section, except in any action brought to enforce the original judgment of the court.

Civil Service Reform Act of 1978

The Civil Service Reform Act of 1978, 5 U.S.C. § 5596(b)(1)(A)(ii), provides:

> An employee of an agency who ... is found ... to have been affected by an unjustified or unwarranted personnel action. ... is entitled, on correction of the personnel action, to receive ... reasonable attorney fees related to the personnel action which, with respect to any decision relating to an unfair labor practice or grievance processed under a procedure negotiated in accordance with chapter 71 of this title, or under chapter 11 of title I of the Foreign Service Act of 1980, shall be awarded in accordance with standards established under section 7701(g) of this title.

Section 7701(g) provides:

> Except as provided in paragraph (2) of this subsection, the [Merit Systems Protection] Board, or an administrative law judge or other employee of the Board designated to hear a case, may require payment by the agency involved of reasonable attorney fees... if warranted in the interest of justice... .
> If an employee or applicant for employment is the prevailing party and the decision is based on a finding of discrimination prohibited under section 2302(b) of this title, the payment of attorney fees shall be in accordance with the standards prescribed under section 706(k) of the Civil Rights Act of 1964 (42 U.S.C. 2000e-5(k)).

Section 2302(b)provides:

> Any employee who has authority to take, direct others to take, recommend, or approve any personnel action, shall not, with respect to such authority — (1) discriminate for or against any employee or applicant for employment—
>
> (A) on the basis of race, color, religion, sex, or national origin, as prohibited under section 717 of the Civil Rights Act of 1964 (42 U.S.C. 2000e-16);
> (B) on the basis of age, as prohibited under sections 12 and 15 of the Age Discrimination in Employment Act of 1967 (29 U.S.C. 631, 633a);
> (C) on the basis of sex, as prohibited by section 6(d) of the Fair Labor Standards Act of 1938 (29 U.S.C. 206(d));

(D) on the basis of handicapping conditions, as prohibited under section 501 of the Rehabilitation Act of 1973 (29 U.S.C. 791); or
(E) on the basis of marital status or political affiliation as prohibited under any law, rule, or regulation.

Thus, in the ordinary case, fees may be awarded if "warranted in the interest of justice," but in civil rights cases the standards of 42 U.S.C. § 2000e-5(k) are incorporated, which apparently means that a prevailing plaintiff should recover fees "in all but very unusual circumstances." *Albemarle Paper Co. v. Moody,* 422 U.S. 405, 415 (1975).[52]

Age Discrimination Act of 1975

The Age Discrimination Act of 1975, 42 U.S.C. §§ 6101 et seq., prohibits age discrimination in programs or activities receiving federal, financial assistance. Public Law 95-478, § 401, amended 42 U.S.C. § 6104(e) to provide that "the Court shall award the costs of suit, including a reasonable attorney's fee, to the prevailing plaintiff."

Civil Rights of Institutionalized Persons Act

Section 3 of the Civil Rights of Institutionalized Persons Act, 42 U.S.C. § I 997a, provides that the Attorney General may institute a civil action against any state or political subdivision of a state or employee thereof whom he has reasonable cause to believe is engaging in a pattern or practice of subjecting persons residing in or confined to an institution (which includes, among other things, mental institutions, prisons, and nursing homes) to egregious or flagrant conditions which deprive such persons of any rights, privileges, or immunities conferred by the Constitution or laws of the United States. In any such action, "the court may allow the prevailing party, other than the United States, a reasonable attorney's fee against the United States as part of the costs." 42 U.S.C. § 1997a(b).

Section 5 of the Act, 42 U.S.C. § 1997c, provides that the Attorney General may intervene in any private action commenced in any federal court seeking relief from a pattern or practice of egregious or flagrant conditions which deprive persons in institutions of any rights, privileges, or immunities secured by the Constitution or laws of the United States. (This section does not appear to create a new private right of action; rather, it contemplates actions under existing law, such as 42 U.S.C. § 1983.) Section 5(d) reads:

52 *See*, Annotation, *Attorneys' Fees Under Back Pay Act* (5 USCS § 5596), 122 ALR Fed 465.

In any action in which the United States joins as an intervenor under this section, the court may allow the prevailing party, other than the United States, a reasonable attorney's fee against the United States as part of the costs. Nothing in this subsection precludes the award of attorney's fees available under any other provisions of the United States Code.

The conference report that accompanied this law explains:

In both the initiation and intervention sections, the Act makes clear the liability of the United States to opposing parties for attorneys' fees whenever it loses. The award is discretionary with the court, and it is intended that the present standards used by courts under the civil rights laws will apply. However, it is not intended that recovery be allowed from the United States, as a plaintiff, by another plaintiff or plaintiff-intervenor. The award is to be made to an opposing party who prevails.[53]

Thus, in actions instituted by or intervened in by the Attorney General, fees may be awarded against the United States only to prevailing defendants, and only if the suit was, in the words of *Christiansburg, supra,* 434 U.S. at 421, "frivolous, unreasonable, or without foundation." Prevailing plaintiffs, other than the United States, apparently may recover attorneys' fees against defendants if awards are authorized under a statute such as the Civil Rights Attorney's Fees Awards Act of 1976 or the common law bad faith exception to the American rule.

In 1996, the Prison Litigation Reform Act, Public Law 104-134, § 803, amended § 7 of the Civil Rights of Institutionalized Persons Act, 42 U.S .C. § 1 997e, to provide that no prisoner may bring an action with respect to prison conditions, under 42 U.S.C. § 1983 or any other federal law, "until such administrative remedies as are available are exhausted." It also limited the right to recover attorneys' fees under the Civil Rights Attorney's Fees Awards Act of 1976, 42 U.S.C. § 1988(b), as detailed below in the discussion of that statute.

Rehabilitation Act of 1973

Section 501 of the Rehabilitation Act of 1973 provides protection from employment discrimination on the basis of handicap by federal executive branch agencies. 29 U.S.C § 791. Section 504, as amended in 1978, prohibits discrimination solely by reason of handicap under programs receiving federal financial assistance or under programs conducted by executive agencies or by the Postal Service. 29 U.S.C. § 794. Section 505, which was added in 1978 provides that specified remedies procedures and rights set forth in Title VII of the Civil Rights Act of 1964 shall be

53 H.Rept. 96-897, 96th Cong., 2d Sess. 12-13 (1980), *reprinted in* 1980 U.S.C.C.A.N. 832, 837.

available with respect to complaints under § 501, and the remedies, procedures and rights set forth in Title VI of the Civil Rights Act of 1964 shall be available with respect to complaints under § 504. Section 505 also provides that in any "action or proceeding" under the Rehabilitation Act, "the court, in its discretion may allow the prevailing party, other than the United States, a reasonable attorney's fee as part of the costs." 29 U.S.C. § 794a.

Individuals with Disabilities Education Act

An attorneys' fees provision was added to the Education of the Handicapped Act by the Handicapped Children's Protection Act of 1986, Public Law 99-372, 20 U.S.C. § 1415(e)(4). This statute was enacted to overturn *Smith v. Robinson,* 468 U.S. 992 (1984), which precluded fee awards under the EHA. The plaintiffs in *Smith v. Robinson* had sued on behalf of a handicapped child who allegedly had been deprived of his right to a free special education. They had sued under state law and under three federal statutes: EHA, § 504 of the Rehabilitation Act of 1973 (29 U.S .C. § 794), and 42 U.S.C. § 1983. The EHA guarantees the right to a free appropriate public education in states that receive grants under the statute; the Rehabilitation Act prohibits discrimination on the basis of handicap in any program or activity that receives federal financial assistance; and § 1983 permits suits against state or local officials if, under color of state law, they deprive someone of a federal constitutional or statutory right.

The EHA prior to the 1986 Act did not authorize awards of attorneys' fees, but the Rehabilitation Act did, and 42 U.S.C. § 1988(b) permits fee awards in § 1983 cases. The plaintiffs in *Smith v. Robinson,* after prevailing on the merits of their case, asked the court to award fees pursuant to either the Rehabilitation Act or § 1988(b). The Supreme Court held that they were not entitled to relief under the Rehabilitation Act or § 1983, and therefore were not entitled to a fee award under either statute. Although these statutes on their face appear to apply to cases of handicapped children who are denied their right to a free appropriate public education, the Court found that, in cases in which these statutes do not provide rights greater than those available under the EHA, Congress intended the EHA to be the exclusive remedy.

Congress, therefore, added 20 U.S.C. § 1415(i)(3)(B) to the EHA, which, as amended by Public Law 105-17, provides:

> In any action or proceeding brought under this subsection, the court, in its discretion, may award reasonable attorneys' fees as part of the costs to the parents of a child with a disability who is the prevailing party.

Administrative proceedings are mandatory under the EHA, and the legislative history makes clear that courts may award fees incurred at the administrative and the judicial levels, including when a party prevails at the administrative level and brings a court action solely to recover fees. Therefore, the Supreme Court's decisions in neither *Webb* nor *Crest Street* appear to preclude a court from awarding attorneys' fees incurred at the administrative level. The attorneys' fees provision prohibits bonuses and multipliers *(see,* pp. 47-52, *infra),* and contains a section based on Rule 68 of the Federal Rules of Civil Procedure *(see,* pp. 53-54, *infra).*[54]

Americans with Disabilities Act of 1990

The ADA, 42 U.S.C. §§ 12101 *et seq.,* provides protection against discrimination on the basis of disability in employment, public services, public accommodations, and telecommunications. It supplements the Rehabilitation Act of 1973 by extending such protection, to varying degrees, to Congress and the legislative branch agencies, to the states,[55] and to the private sector. Section 505 of the ADA, 42 U.S.C. § 12205, provides:

> In any action or administrative proceeding commenced pursuant to this Act, the court or agency, in its discretion, may allow the prevailing party, other than the United States, a reasonable attorney's fee, including litigation expenses, and costs, and the United States shall be liable for the foregoing the same as a private individual.

Civil Rights Attorney's Fees Awards Act of 1976

The Civil Rights Attorney's Fees Awards Act of 1976, 42 U.S.C. § 1988(b), provides:

> In any action or proceeding to enforce a provision of sections 1981, 1981a, 1982, 1983, 1985, and 1986 of this title, title IX of Public Law 92-318, the Religious Freedom Restoration Act of 1993, the Religious Land Use and Institutionalized Persons Act of 2000, title VI of the Civil Rights Act of 1964, or section 40302 of the

---

54 For additional information, *see, Individuals with Disabilities Education Act: Awards of Attorneys' Fees* (CRS Report No. 96-873 A, Nov. 1, 1996), although this report was written prior to the enactment of Public Law 104-17 (1997). That law's two substantive changes to the attorneys' fees section were to provide: (1) "Attorneys' fees may not be awarded relating to any meeting of the IEP [individualized educational program] Team unless such meeting is convened as a result of an administrative proceeding or judicial action, or, at the discretion of the State, for a mediation... ," and (2) "whenever the court finds that... the attorney representing the parent did not provide to the school district the appropriate information in the due process complaint... . The court shall reduce, accordingly, the amount of the attorneys' fees awarded under this section."

55 Eleventh Amendment immunity, which is discussed at pp. 40-45, *infra,* is explicitly waived by § 502 of the ADA, 42 U.S.C. § 12202.

Violence Against Women Act of 1994, the court, in its discretion, may allow the prevailing party, other than the United States, a reasonable attorney's fee as part of the costs, except that in any action brought against a judicial officer for an act or omission taken in such officer's judicial capacity such officer shall not be held liable for any costs, including attorney's fees, unless such action was clearly in excess of such officer's jurisdiction.[56]

In 1996, the Prison Litigation Reform Act, Public Law 104-134, § 803, amended § 7 of the Civil Rights of Institutionalized Persons Act, 42 U.S.C. § I 997e(d), to provide:

(1) In any action brought by a prisoner... fees shall not be awarded [under § 1988 (b)], except to the extent that —
(A) the fee was directly and reasonably incurred in proving an actual violation of the plaintiff's rights protected by a statute pursuant to which a fee may be awarded under [§ 1988(b)]; and
(B)(i) the amount of the fee is proportionately related to the court ordered relief for the violation; or (ii) the fee was directly and reasonably incurred in enforcing the relief ordered for the violation.

(2) Whenever a monetary judgment is awarded in an action described in paragraph (1), a portion of the judgment (not to exceed 25 percent) shall be applied to satisfy the amount of attorney's fees awarded against the defendant. If the award of attorney's fees is not greater than 150 percent of the judgment, the excess shall be paid by the defendant.

(3) No award of attorney's fees in an action described in paragraph (1) shall be based on an hourly rate greater than 150 percent of the hourly rate established under section 3006A of title 18, United States Code, for payment of court-appointed counsel.
(4) Nothing in this subsection shall prohibit a prisoner from entering into an agreement to pay an attorney's fee in an amount greater than the amount authorized under this subsection....

In *Martin v. Hadix,* 527 U.S. 343 (1999), the Supreme Court held that 42 U.S.C. § 1997e(d)(3) "limits attorney's fees with respect to post judgment monitoring services performed after the PLRA's [Prison Litigation Reform Act's] effective date but it does not so limit fees for post judgment monitoring performed before the effective date."

The ten statutes under which § 1988(b) authorizes fee awards are now examined in the order § 1988(b) lists them.

---

56 As for the citation of this statute, *see,* note 10, *supra.* Cases under § 1988(b) are collected at 43 ALR Fed 243, 69 ALR Fed 712, and 118 ALR Fed 1. The exception for judicial officers was added by

42 U.S.C. § 1981

This section provides:

> All persons within the jurisdiction of the United States shall have the same right in every State and Territory to make and enforce contracts, to sue, be parties, give evidence, and to the full and equal benefit of all laws and proceedings for the security of persons and property as is enjoyed by white citizens, and shall be subject to like punishment, pains, penalties, taxes, licenses, and exactions of every kind, and to no other.

42 U.S.C. § 1981a

This section, enacted by the Civil Rights Act of 1991, Public Law 102-166, § 102, provides for punitive damages in actions for unlawful intentional employment discrimination under specified statutes.

42 U.S.C. § 1982

This section provides:

> All citizens of the United States shall have the same right, in every State and Territory, as is enjoyed by white citizens thereof to inherit, purchase, lease, sell, hold, and convey real and personal property.

42 U.S.C. § 1983

This section provides:

> Every person who, under color of any statute, ordinance, regulation, custom, or usage, of any State or Territory, subjects, or causes to be subjected, any citizen of the United States or other person within the jurisdiction thereof to the deprivation of any rights, privileges, or immunities secured by the Constitution, and laws, shall be liable to the party injured in an action at law, suit in equity, or other proper proceeding for redress, except that in any action brought against a judicial officer for an act or omission taken in such officer's judicial capacity, injunctive relief shall not be granted unless a declaratory decree was violated or declaratory relief was unavailable. For the purposes of this section, any Act of Congress applicable exclusively to the District of Columbia shall be considered to be a statute of the District of Columbia.[57]

Section 1983 permits suits against state and local officials, as individuals, if, under color of state law, they deprive someone of a federally protected right. The

---

Public Law 104-317, § 309(b), and is discussed at p. 44, *infra*.

[57] The exception for judicial officers was added by Public Law 104-317, § 309(c).

Supreme Court has held that a state is not a "person" subject to suit under § 1983. *Will v. Michigan Department of State Police,* 491 U.S. 58 (1989). Furthermore, a suit for damages against a state official acting in his or her official capacity "is no different from a suit against the State itself." *Id.* at 71.

However, "a State official in his or her official capacity, when sued for injunctive relief, would be a person under § 1983 because 'official-capacity actions for prospective relief are not treated as actions against the State.'" *Id.* at 71 n.10. In such suits, attorneys' fees may be awarded against a state under § 1988b, but not against the state official personally, except under the common law bad faith standard. *Hutto v. Finney,* 437 U.S. 678, 692 n.19, 693, 700 (1978) (discussed in detail in section IX of this report).

State officials may be sued in their individual capacities for damages under § 1983. *Hafer v. Melo,* 502 U.S. 21 (1991). In such suits, a state official may be held liable for attorneys' fees even in the absence of bad faith. However, the state will not be liable for fees. *Kentucky v. Graham,* 473 U.S. 159 (1985).

Section 1983 permits suits against local governments, provided that the deprivation of rights was based on official policy and not merely respondent superior (the common law liability of employers for acts of employees). *Monell v. Department of Social Services of the City of New York,* 436 U.S. 658 (1978). If a local official is sued under § 1983 in his official capacity, the public entity is liable "provided of course, the public entity received notice and an opportunity to respond" *Brandor v. Holt,* 469 U.S. 464, 471-472 (1985).

Maine v. Thiboutot 448 U.S. (b) 1980 was a case brought under § 1983 of a state court challenging the state's method of computing benefits under a federally-funded public assistance program. The state argued that § 1983 does not provide for suits brought to enforce purely statutory, non-constitutional claims, but the Supreme Court held that "the phrase 'and laws,' as used in § 1983, means what it says." Id. at 4. In other words, according to this case, suits may be brought under § 1983 to enforce statutory as well as constitutional claims — even statutory claims unrelated to civil rights and even claims arising under statutes that do not themselves contain an express or implied private right of action. And, the Court held, under § 1988(b), state as well as federal courts may award attorneys' fees in § 1983 suits.[58]

In *Dennis v. Higgins,* 498 U.S. 439 (1991), the Supreme Court held that suits against state officials for violation of the Commerce Clause (Art. I, § 8, cl. 3) may be brought under § 1983. The Court found that the Commerce Clause confers a right "to

---

58 Subsequently, the Supreme Court limited the scope of *Thiboutot,* finding exceptions to the rule that § 1983 provides a cause of action for violations of federal statutes as well as the Constitution. *See, e.g.,* Livadas v. Bradshaw, 512 U.S. 107, 132 (1994): Suter v. Artist M., 503 U.S. 347, 355 (1992); Wilder v. Virginia Hospital Association, 496 U.S. 498, 508 (1990); Middlesex County Sewerage Authority v. National Sea Clammters Association, 453 U.S. 1, 20 (1981); Pennhurst State School and Hospital v. Halderman, 451 U.S. 1, 15 (1981).

engage in interstate trade free from restrictive state regulation" *(id.* at 448), and that this right is protected by § 1983.

There may be another limitation upon awards of attorneys' fees under § 1988(b) in § 1983 cases. *In Maher v. Gagne,* 448 U.S. 122 (1980), which the Supreme Court decided the same day as *Thiboutot,* the Court left open the question whether the Eleventh Amendment prohibits federal courts from awarding fees in wholly-statutory, non-civil rights cases. The impact of the Eleventh Amendment on fee awards against the states is considered in section IX of this report, but brief mention of it will be made here in order to explain more fully the holdings of *Maine v. Thiboutot* and *Maher v. Gagne.*

The Eleventh Amendment generally prohibits suits for damages in federal court against a state. Notwithstanding the Eleventh Amendment, however, a state may be sued for damages in federal court for violations of laws enacted to enforce the Fourteenth Amendment. Section 1983, and civil rights laws generally, were enacted to enforce the Fourteenth Amendment. *Maine v. Thiboutot,* however, held that § 1983 permits assertion of claims arising under both civil rights and non-civil rights laws. This raises the question whether claims arising under non-civil rights laws should be considered as having been brought under a law enacted to enforce the Fourteenth Amendment merely because the laws under which they arise may be enforced through the use of § 1983. The Court did not have to answer this question in *Maine v, Thiboutot* because that case was brought in state court, where the Eleventh Amendment does not apply.

Maher v. Gagne the Court also avoided the question, but for a different reason. This case was brought in federal court, and, like *Maine v. Thihoutot,* it charged a state with having violated a non-civil rights law. However, the plaintiff in *Maher v. Gagne* also raised a constitutional claim, and that was decisive. Prior to trial, the case was settled favorably for the plaintiff, without the constitutional issue's being reached. The state argued that the Eleventh Amendment prohibited a fee award because the case involved a purely statutory, non-civil rights claim. The Court held, however, that, under § 1988(b), a federal court, notwithstanding the Eleventh Amendment, may award attorneys' "fees in a case in which the plaintiff prevails on a wholly statutory, non-civil rights claim pendent to a substantial constitutional claim or in one in which both a statutory and a substantial constitutional claim are settled favorably to the plaintiff without adjudication." *Id.* at 132. Because of the constitutional claim (which was held to be substantial), the Court found "there is no need to reach the question whether a federal court could award attorney's fees against a State based on a statutory, non-civil-rights claim." *Id.* at 130.[59]

---

[59] *See,* note 69, *infra.*

42 U.S.C. § 1985

This section has three subsections. Subsection (a) gives to "any person" a right to be free from a conspiracy "to prevent, by force, intimidation, or threat" the acceptance of a federal office" or from discharging any duties thereof." Subsection (b) gives any person who is a party or a witness, or a grand or petit juror, in any court of the United States a right to be free from a conspiracy to obstruct justice. Subsection (c) protects persons from deprivations "of equal protection of the laws, or of equal privileges and immunities under the laws."

42 U.S.C. § 1986

This section provides that any person who has knowledge that any of the wrongs mentioned in 42 U.S.C. § 1985 are about to be committed, and has the power to prevent or aid in preventing the commission of such wrongs, who neglects or refuses so to do, shall be liable to the party injured for all damages caused by the wrongful act which such person by reasonable diligence could have prevented.

Title IX of Public Law 92-318

This statute, codified at 20 U.S.C. §§ 1681 *et seq.*, prohibits discrimination on the basis of sex, blindness, or severe visual impairment under any educational program or activity receiving federal assistance. In *Cannon v. University of Chicago,* 441 U.S. 667 (1979), the Supreme Court held that Title IX contains an implied private right of action. In *Franklin v. Gwinnett County Public Schools,* 503 U.S. 60 (1992), the Court added that this right includes the remedy of monetary damages.

Religious Freedom Restoration Act of 1993

This statute (Public Law 103-141, 42 U.S.C. §§ 2000bb *et seq.*) was enacted in response to *Employment Division, Oregon Department of Human Resources v. Smith,* 494 U.S. 872 (1990), in which the Supreme Court held that religiously neutral laws (in this case a law proscribing the use of peyote) usually may be applied without regard to any burden they place on the exercise of religion. In other words, the First Amendment's guarantee of the free exercise of religion ordinarily mandates no religious exemptions from otherwise valid laws. The Religious Freedom Restoration Act provides statutory protection in leu of constitutional protection. It prohibits government at all levels from substantially burdening a person's exercise of religion unless the government demonstrates that the burden is in furtherance of a compelling governmental interest and is the least restrictive means of furthering that interest. The Act contains an express private right of action.[60]

The Religious Land Use and Institutionalized Persons Act of 2000

This statute (Public Law 106-274, 42 U.S.C. §§ 2000cc *et seq.*) provides that "[n]o [state or local] government shall impose or implement a land use regulation in a manner that imposes a substantial burden on the religious exercise of a person, including a religious assembly or institution, unless the government demonstrates that imposition of the burden on that person, assembly, or institution— (A) is in furtherance of a compelling governmental interest; and (B) is the least restrictive means of furthering that compelling governmental interest." This prohibition applies if the burden is imposed in a program or activity that receives federal financial assistance. affects interstate commerce, or is imposed through a process that permits the government to make individualized assessments of the proposed uses for the property involved.

The statute also provides that "[n]o [state or local] government shall impose a substantial burden on the religious exercise of a person residing in or confined to an institution, as defined in section 2 of the Civil Rights of Institutionalized Persons Act (42 U.S.C. 1997)... unless the government demonstrates that imposition of the burden on that person — (1) is in furtherance of a compelling governmental interest; and (2) is the least restrictive means of furthering that compelling governmental interest." This prohibition applies if the burden is imposed in a program or activity that receives federal financial assistance or affects interstate commerce.

The statute also provides that "[n]o [state or local] government shall impose or implement a land use regulation in a manner that treats a religious assembly or institution on less than equal terms with a non religious assembly or institution," or "that discriminates against any assembly or institution on the basis of religion or religious denomination."

Civil Rights Act of 1964, Title VI — Federally Assisted Programs

This statute, codified at 42 U.S.C. § 2000d *et seq.*, provides:

> No person in the United States shall, on the ground of race, color, or national origin, be excluded from participation in, be denied the benefits of, or be subjected to discrimination under any program or activity receiving Federal financial assistance.

---

60 *See, The Religious Freedom Restoration Act: Its Rise, Fall, and Current Status* (CR5 Report No. 97-795 A). In *City of Boerne v. Flores,* 521 U.S. 507 (1997), the Supreme Court declared RFRA unconstitutional as applied to the states, on the ground that Congress had exceeded its power under § 5 of the Fourteenth Amendment in applying it to the states.

In *Guardians Association v. Civil Service Commission of the City of New York* 463 U.S. 582 (1983), a majority of the Justices indicated that Title VI contains a private right of action.

Violence Against Women Act of 1994

Section 40302 of this Act provides that "[a] person... who commits a crime of violence motivated by gender... shall be liable to the party injured, in an action for the recovery of compensatory and punitive damages, injunctive and declaratory relief, and such other relief as a court may deem appropriate."[61]

AWARDS OF ATTORNEYS' FEES IN TAX CASES

Section 7430 of the Internal Revenue Code, 26 U.S.C. § 7430, authorizes the Internal Revenue Service and federal courts to award attorneys' fees of up to $125 an hour in tax cases in which the United States fails to establish that its position in the proceedings was substantially justified. In this respect, § 7430 is similar to EAJA, discussed at page 6, *supra.* In other respects, however, it is different, and the law governing awards of attorneys' fees in tax eases has undergone multiple changes since Congress first authorized fee-shifting in tax cases in 1976.

Awards of attorneys' fees in tax cases were first permitted by the Civil Rights Attorney's Fees Awards Act of 1976, 42 U.S.C. § 1988(b), which authorized federal courts to award attorneys' fees to a prevailing party, other than the United States, "in any civil action or proceeding, by or on behalf of the United States of America, to enforce, or charging a violation of, a provision of the United States Internal Revenue Code." This provision, commonly known as the "Allen amendment," had little effect because of its limitation to tax cases brought "by or on behalf of the United States." Although in several circumstances the United States may bring suit under the Internal Revenue Code, in the vast majority of tax cases the taxpayer is the plaintiff. See Key *Buick Company v. Commissioner of Internal Revenue,* 613 F.2d 1306 (5th Cir. 1980). Even in those cases that are brought by or on behalf of the United States in which the taxpayer is the defendant, a prevailing defendant is entitled to fees under § 1988(b) only upon a finding that the action is "meritless in the sense that it is groundless or without foundation." *Hughes v. Rowe,* 449 U.S. 5, 14 (1980).

---

61 Section 40302 is part of the Civil Rights Remedies for Gender-Motivated Violence Act, which is Subtitle C of the Violence Against Women Act of 1994, which is part of Title IV of the Violent Crime Control and Law Enforcement Act of 1994, Public Law 103-322.

The Equal Access to Justice Act (EAJA), which took effect October 1, 1981, amended § 1988(b) to remove its authorization for awards of attorneys' fees in tax cases. EAJA instead itself authorized federal courts to award attorneys' fees against the United States in tax cases, except those brought in Tax Court. This exception had not been explicit in the Act, but a committee report indicated that the courts empowered by the Act to award attorneys' fees "are those defined in section 451 of title 28," and the Tax Court is not among them.[62] Apart from this, awards of attorneys' fees in tax eases could be awarded under the same conditions as other awards against the United States under the EAJA: a prevailing plaintiff whose net worth was within the prescribed limits was entitled to an award up to $75 per hour (or more if a special factor justified a higher fee) unless the United States proved that its position was substantially justified or that special circumstances made an award unjust.

Next, § 292 of the Tax Equity and Fiscal Responsibility Act of 1982 (TEFRA), Public Law 97-248, made the EAJA inapplicable to tax cases and enacted § 7430 of the Internal Revenue Code. Section 7430 authorized fee awards in federal courts, including Tax Court, placed a cap of $25,000 on fee awards, and authorized awards only if the taxpayer proved that the position of the United States was "unreasonable," it contained no limits on hourly rates or the net worth of eligible plaintiffs. Section 7430 sunset, but was reenacted with amendments by § 1551 of the Tax Reform Act of 1986, Public Law 99-514. Then, in 1988, Public Law 100-647, § 6239, amended § 7430 to apply in administrative, as well as court, proceedings.

The 1986 Act, while not placing tax cases back within the EAJA, amended § 7430 to make it more like the EAJA. Section 7430, as amended in 1988 and 1996, provides that, in any administrative or court proceeding brought by or against the United States, in connection with the determination, collection, or refund of any tax, interest, or penalty under the Internal Revenue Code, the prevailing party, other than the United States or a creditor of the taxpayer, may be awarded litigation costs, including reasonable attorneys' fees. Section 7430 contains the same limitations as the EAJA on the net worth of eligible plaintiffs (see § 7430(c)(4)(A)(ii), as renumbered by Public Law 104-168, § 701(a)), and it originally contained the same $75 cap on hourly rates. However, in 1996, Public Law 104-121 raised EAJA's rate to $125, and Public Law 104-168, § 702, raised § 7430's to $110, with cost of living increases after 1996. In 1998, Public Law 105-206, § 3101, raised § 7430's cap to $125, without amending the language authorizing cost of living increases after 1996.

As under the EAJA, a party is not eligible for a fee award "if the United States establishes that the position of the United States in the proceeding was substantially justified." 26 U.S.C. § 7430(c)(4)(B)(i). (Prior to enactment of this provision by Public Law 104-168, § 701(b), the burden of proof as to this issue was on the

---

[62] H.Rept. 96-1418, 96th Cong., 2d Sess. 17 (1980), *reprinted in* 1980 U.S.C.C.A.N. 4984, 4996.

taxpayer.) Unlike the EAJA, § 7430 does not allow the government to avoid a fee award where "special circumstances make an award unjust."

Section 6673 (a) of the Internal Revenue Code, 26 U.S.C. § 6673(a), as amended by Public Law 101-239, § 7731(a), allows the Tax Court to impose upon a taxpayer a penalty of up to $25,000 if it finds that —

A. proceedings before it have been instituted or maintained by the taxpayer primarily for delay,
B. the taxpayer's position in such proceedings is frivolous or groundless, or
C. the taxpayer unreasonably failed to pursue available administrative remedies.

Section 6673(a) also allows the Tax Court to require any attorney who unreasonably and vexatiously multiplies the proceedings in any ease to pay personally the excess costs, expenses, and attorneys' fees reasonably incurred because of such conduct. If the attorney is appearing on behalf of the IRS, then the United States must pay the amount awarded.

Section 6673(b) allows the court to impose upon a taxpayer a penalty of up to $10,000 "[w]henever it appears to the court that the taxpayer's position in proceedings... under section 7433 is frivolous or groundless...." Section 7433 authorizes taxpayers to sue the United States in federal district court if an Internal Revenue Service officer or employee "recklessly or intentionally disregards" any provision of the Internal Revenue Code. Under § 7433, a prevailing taxpayer may recover up to $100,000 of "(1) actual, direct economic damages sustained as a proximate result of the reckless or intentional actions of the officer or employee, and (2) the costs of the action." Awards of attorneys' fees are already provided for by § 7430.

Awards of Attorneys' Fees against the States

Article III, § 2, of the United States Constitution provides that the judicial power of the United States *(i.e.,* federal court jurisdiction) shall extend to controversies between a state and citizens of another state. The Eleventh Amendment modifies this section by providing that the judicial power of the United States shall not be construed to extend to any suit against a state by citizens of another state or of a foreign state. In *Hans v. Louisiana,* 134 U.S. 1 (1890), the Supreme Court construed the Eleventh Amendment to prohibit a citizen from suing even his own state in federal court.[63] In

[63] Dissenting in *Dellmuth v. Muth,* 491 U.S. 223, 233 (1989), Justices Brennan, Marshall, Blackmun, and Stevens expressed the view that *Hans v. Louisiana* should be overruled.

Alden v. Maine, 527 U.S. 706 (1999), the Supreme Court held that the Eleventh Amendment prevents Congress from authorizing private suits against a state, even in its own courts, without the state's consent. Notwithstanding the Eleventh Amendment, a state may consent to suit by its citizens or citizens of other states. *Missouri v. Fiske,* 290 U.S. 18, 24 (1933).

In *Ex parte Young,* 209 U.S. 123 (1908), the Supreme Court held that federal courts may enjoin state officials as individuals from enforcing state laws that violate the United States Constitution.[64] The Court reasoned that an official who attempts such action "comes into conflict with the superior authority of that Constitution, and he is in that case stripped of his official or representative character and is subject in his person to the consequences of his individual conduct." *Id.* at 159-160. One commentator noted:

> The idea that the court restrained the individual rather than the state was, of course, pure fiction, since the state could not act other than through its officials. But through this fiction the Court apparently sought to guarantee the nation's authority to limit state action.[65]

In *Edelnmn v. Jordan,* 415 U.S. 651 (1974), the Supreme Court explicitly limited the types of relief that may be granted under the theory of *Ex parte Young.* The plaintiffs in *Edehnan* had sued state officials, alleging that the officials were administering a welfare program in a manner inconsistent with various federal regulations. The district court found for the plaintiffs and ordered the state officials to comply with federal regulations in the future and to disburse all benefits wrongfully withheld in the past. The court of appeals affirmed. The Supreme Court affirmed the prospective portion of the district courts order, but reversed the retroactive portion of the order, holding that because the award must inevitably come from the general revenues of the State of Illinois," it "resembles far more closely the monetary award against the State itself... than it does the prospective injunctive relief awarded in *Ex parte Young." Id,* at 665. The Court acknowledged that "the difference between the type of relief barred by the Eleventh Amendment and that permitted under *Ex parte Young* will not in many instances be that between day and night." *Id.* at 667. This is evidenced by the fact that the prospective portion of the district court's order, as well as the retroactive portion, necessarily required the payment of state funds, but this the Court termed a permissible "ancillary effect" of the prospective order.[66]

---

64 In subsequent cases, the Court has indicated that federal courts may also enjoin state officials from enforcing state laws that violate federal laws or regulations. *See, e.g., Edehnan v. Jordan,* in the text below.

65 *Attorneys' Fees and the Eleventh Amendment,* 88 Harvard Law Review 1875, 1879 (1975).

66 In *Pennhurst State School & Hospital v. Halderman,* 465 U.S. 89, 106, 121 (1984), the Supreme Court held "that *Young* and *Edelman* are inapplicable in a suit against state officials on the basis of state law. ...[T]his principle applies as well to state-law claims brought into federal court under

In Fitzpatrick v. Bitzer, 427 U.S. 445, 456 (1976), the Supreme Court lessened the importance of its ruling in *Edelman by* holding that the Eleventh Amendment is "necessarily limited by the enforcement provisions of § 5 of the Fourteenth Amendment." In *Fitzpatrick* the plaintiffs had sued a state official under Title VII of the Civil Rights Act of 1964, which was enacted under § 5 of the Fourteenth Amendment and which includes a fee-shifting provision. Like the plaintiffs in *Edelman,* the plaintiffs in *Fitzpatrick* had sought prospective injunctive relief and retroactive benefits; in addition, in *Fitzpatrick* they had sought attorneys' fees. The district court awarded only the prospective relief holding that the other relief was barred by *Edelman.* The court of appeals agreed that *Edelman* barred an award of retroactive benefits, but held that an award of attorneys' fees was a permissible ancillary benefit.

The Supreme Court did not decide whether an award of attorneys' fees constituted an impermissible retroactive benefit or a permissible ancillary benefit. Instead, it reversed the denial of retroactive benefits, holding that neither they nor an award of attorneys' fees were barred in situations in which Congress, under § 5 of the Fourteenth Amendment, had provided for suits against states or state officials. The Supreme Court held, in other words, that the constitutional power of Congress to enforce "by appropriate legislation" the Fourteenth Amendment was intended to supersede the Eleventh Amendment and allow congressionally authorized suits (and awards of attorneys' fees) against both states and state officials.

In *Atascadero State Hospital v. Scanlon,* 473 U.S. 234, 242 (1985), the Supreme Court held "that Congress may abrogate the States' constitutionally secured immunity from suit in federal court only by making its intention unmistakably clear in the language of the statute." Subsequently, Congress made explicit that states are not immune under the Eleventh Amendment from suits in federal court under any "Federal statute prohibiting discrimination by recipients of Federal financial assistance." 42 U.S.C. § 2000d-7.[67]

---

pendent jurisdiction." In other words, the Eleventh Amendment prohibits a state-law claim against state officials from being brought in federal court, even if it is joined with a federal-law claim. This has caused some state courts to refuse to "hear claims under 42 U.S.C. § 1983 (1982) that seek an award of attorney's fees under the Civil Rights Attorney's Fees Awards Act of 1976 (Section 1988)." Wilbur, *Concurrent Jurisdiction and Attorney's Fees: The Obligation of State Courts to Hear Section 1983 Claims,* 134 University of Pennsylvania Law Review 1207 (1986).

67 In *Dellmuth v. Muth,* 491 U.S. 223, 232 (1989), the Court held that the Education of the Handicapped Act, did "not evince an unmistakably clear intention to abrogate the States' constitutionally secured immunity from suit [in federal court]." This decision apparently applied only to suits alleging violations that occurred before 42 U.S.C. § 2000d-7 took effect in 1986. *See, id.* at 228-229. Yet, in 1990, Public Law 101-476, § 103, amended the Education of the Handicapped Act to provide, effective Oct. 30, 1990: "A State shall not be immune under the eleventh amendment to the Constitution of the United States from suit in Federal court for a violation of this Act." 20 U.S.C. § 1403. A committee report states that this was intended to overturn *Dellmuth v. Muth.* H.Rept. 101-544, 101st Cong., 2d Sess. 12; *reprinted in* 1990 U.S.C.C.A.N. 1723, 1734.

In *Pennsylvania v. Union Gas Co.,* 491 U.S. 1 (1989), the Supreme Court held that Congress also has the authority to override states' Eleventh Amendment immunity when legislating pursuant to the Commerce Clause. However, in *Seminole Tribe of Florida v. Florida,* 517 U.S. 44, 72 (1996), the Supreme Court overruled *Pennsylvania v. Union Gas Co.,* writing: "Even when the Constitution vests in Congress complete lawmaking authority over a particular area, the Eleventh Amendment prevents congressional authorization of suits by private parties against unconsenting States." The Court noted, however, that "an individual may [still] obtain injunctive relief under *Ex parte Young* in order to remedy a state officer's ongoing violation of federal law." *Id.* at 72 n.16.

In *Alden v. Maine,* 527 U.S. 706, 712 (1999), the Supreme Court held "that the powers delegated to Congress under Article I of the United States Constitution do not include the power to subject nonconsenting States to private suits for damages instate courts." This decision continues to allow the federal government to sue the states in federal or state courts, and continues to allow private suits for damages in state courts under statutes enacted pursuant to the Fourteenth Amendment.[68]

In *Hutto v. Finney,* 437 U.S. 678 (1978), the Supreme Court affirmed two awards of attorneys' fees against the State of Arkansas: a $20,000 award by a federal district court and a $2,500 award for services on appeal by the Court of Appeals for the Eighth Circuit. The district court based its award on the bad faith exception to the American rule. The court of appeals affirmed this award on the basis of the Civil Rights Attorney's Fees Awards Act of 1976, 42 U.S.C. § 1988(b), which had been enacted while the appeal was pending, although the court of appeals noted that the award would have been justified under the bad faith exception. 548 F.2d 740, 742 n. 6.

Because § 1988(b) is a statute enacted pursuant to § 5 of the Fourteenth Amendment, and *Fitzpatrick* held that the Eleventh Amendment does not apply to such statutes, the Supreme Court apparently could have affirmed the district court fee award in *Hutto* on the basis of § 1988(b) merely by finding that § 1988(b) permitted awards of attorneys' fees against the states. The Court chose, however, to affirm on the basis of the bad faith exception. As the bad faith exception is a common law rule not enacted pursuant to a statute that abrogates Eleventh Amendment immunity, the Court had to address the Eleventh Amendment question. It held that the district court award served the same purpose as a remedial fine imposed for civil contempt and did not constitute a retroactive monetary award, and therefore was not barred by the Eleventh Amendment under *Edelman.*

68 In *Kimel v. Florida Board of Regents,* 120 S. Ct. 631 (2000), the Court held that the Age Discrimination in Employment Act, though a valid exercise of Congress's commerce power, could not be applied to the states unless Congress also had the power to enact it under § 5 of the Fourteenth Amendment, which Congress does not.

In *Missouri v. Jenkins,* 491 U.S. 274,280(1989), the Supreme Court made clear that the "holding of *Hutto*... was not just that Congress had spoken sufficiently clearly to overcome Eleventh Amendment immunity in enacting § 1988, but rather that the Eleventh Amendment did not apply to an award of attorney's fees ancillary to a grant of prospective relief." The holding of *Missouri* was that the Eleventh Amendment also does not apply to the calculation of the amount of a fee award and therefore does not prohibit enhancement of a fee award against a state to compensate for delay in payment.

The $2,500 court of appeals award in *Hutto* was made solely pursuant to § 1988(b), and in affirming this award the Court held that Congress intended § 1988(b) to permit awards of attorneys' fees against the states. The Court based this conclusion on the legislative history of § 1988(b) and on the fact that § 1988(b) provides for fee awards "as part of the costs," and "[c]osts have traditionally been awarded without regard for the States' Eleventh Amendment immunity." *Id.* at 695. The Court also held that fees could be awarded against the state even though the state had not been named as a defendant. "Congress recognized that suits brought against individual officers for injunctive relief are for all practical purposes suits against the state itself." *Id.* at 700.

Thus, in a suit for injunctive relief, the state, not the state official, may be held liable for fees under § 1988(b). However, in a suit for injunctive relief a state official may be assessed fees under the common law bad faith standard, which was not affected by § 1988(b). *Id.* at 692 n.19, 693, 700.

In addition, *in Kentucky v. Graham,* 473 U.S. 159 (1985), the Supreme Court indicated that state officials who are not, like judges (discussed below), immune from damages liability, may be sued in their personal capacities for damages under § 1983, and in such cases may be liable for fees even in the absence of bad faith. In such cases, however, the state will not be liable for fees.

The holding in *Hutto v. Finney* that § 1988(b) permits fee awards against the states took on added importance in 1980, when the Supreme Court expanded the reach of § 1988(b) in *Maine v. Thiboutot* and *Maher v. Gagne,* both of which were discussed in detail in section VI of this report. Briefly, *Maine v. Thiboutot* permitted state courts to award fees in any action against a state for violation of any federal law (although subsequent eases discussed above narrowed this holding), and *Maher v. Gagne* permitted federal courts to do the same, provided there is a substantial claim raised under the Constitution or a statute enacted under § 5 of the Fourteenth Amendment. The Court left open the question whether the Eleventh Amendment allows federal courts to award fees in wholly statutory non-civil rights cases.[69]

---

[69] Although the Supreme Court has not explicitly decided the question, the fact that it held in *Seminole Tribe, supra,* that Congress may not override the Eleventh Amendment when legislating pursuant to the Commerce Clause suggests that § 1988(b) does not apply to § 1983 claims that do not arise under the Fourteenth Amendment.

Awards of Attorneys' Fees Against State Judges

In *Supreme Court of Virginia v. Consumers Union of the United States,* 446 U.S. 719 (1980), and in *Pulliam v. Allen,* 466 U.S. 522 (1984), the issue arose whether state judges, sued in their official capacities under 42 U.S.C. § 1983, enjoy any immunity from awards of attorneys' fees that other state officials lack. The answer, the Court found, depended upon whether the judges were sued for damages or injunctive relief, and whether the conduct concerning which they were sued had been performed in their legislative, enforcement, or adjudicative capacity. In 1996, Public Law 104-317, § 309, modified the law announced in *Pulliam.*

In *Consumers Union,* the Virginia court's restrictions on lawyer advertising were found to violate the First Amendment's guarantee of freedom of speech. The Supreme Court held that in propounding the advertising prohibitions the Virginia court had acted in a legislative capacity, and that in such capacity it enjoys common law immunity from damages liability and from declaratory and injunctive relief; and thus from awards of attorneys' fees. However, the Court noted, although *Consumers Union* had alleged only that the Virginia court had promulgated the advertising prohibitions, the Virginia court, in addition to its legislative function, has adjudicative and enforcement authority in attorney disciplinary cases.

In their adjudicative and enforcement capacities, judges enjoy absolute immunity from damages liability. However, in both these capacities, they are subject to suits for injunctive relief, and, under § 1988(b), to awards of attorneys' fees. *(Consumers Union* held this with respect to courts' enforcement authority, and *Pulliam* held it with respect to their adjudicatory authority.) *In Pulliam,* the Court wrote:

> Petitioner insists that judicial immunity bars a fee award because attorney's fees are the functional equivalent of monetary damages and monetary damages indisputably are prohibited by judicial immunity. She reasons that the chilling effect of a damages award is not less chilling when the award is denominated attorney's fees. There is, perhaps, some logic to petitioner's reasoning. The weakness in it is that it is for Congress, not this Court, to determine whether and to what extent to abrogate the judiciary's common-law immunity. *See Pierson v. Ray,* 386 U.S., at 554. Congress has made clear in § 1988 its intent that attorney's fees be available in any action to enforce a provision of § 1983.

466 U.S. at 543.

It should be emphasized that, under *Puliam* the state and not the judge ordinarily will be liable for attorneys' fees. As noted above, in *Hutto,* the Supreme Court held that, in injunctive suits, the state must pay fees awarded under § 1988(b); state officials may be held personally liable for fees only under the common law bad faith standard.

In 1996, Public Law 104-317, § 309(b), amended 42 U.S.C. § 1988(b) to make judicial officers immune from awards of costs, including attorneys' fees, for any "act or omission taken in such officer's judicial capacity... unless such action was clearly in excess of such officer's jurisdiction." Section 309(a) prescribed the same rule for federal judicial officers who are subject to *Bivens* actions.[70] Section 309(c) amended 42 U.S .C. § 1983 to prohibit injunctive relief against a state judicial officer "unless a declaratory decree was violated or declaratory relief was unavailable."

AWARDS OF COSTS IN FEDERAL COURTS

Federal Rule of Civil Procedure 54(d), 28 U.S.C. App. Rule 54(d*),* defines the power of federal courts to allow costs to prevailing parties. It states:

> Except when express provision therefor is made in a statute of the United States or in these rules, costs shall be allowed as of course to the prevailing party unless the court otherwise directs; but costs against the United States, its officers, and agencies shall be imposed only to the extent permitted by law....

"Costs" that may be awarded are those items enumerated in 28 U.S.C. § 1920, which do not include attorneys' fees. Section 1920 provides that federal courts may tax as costs" (order the losing party to pay) the following:

(1) Fees of the clerk and marshal;
(2) Fees of the court reporter for all or any part of the stenographic transcript necessarily obtained for use in the case;
(3) Fees and disbursements for printing and witnesses;
(4) Fees for exemplification and copies of papers necessarily obtained for use in the case;
(5) Docket fees under section 1923 of this title;
(6) Compensation of court appointed experts, compensation of interpreters, and salaries, fees, expenses, and costs of special interpretation services under section 1828 of this Title.

In *Crawford Fitting Co. v. J.T. Gibbons, Inc.*, 482 U.S. 437, 438 (1987), the Supreme Court "addressed the power of federal courts to require a losing party o pay the compensation of the winner's expert witnesses." The Court held that "a federal court is bound by the limits of [28 U.S.C.] § 1821, absent contract or explicit statutory authority to the contrary." *Id.* at 439. Section 1821, the cited statute, provides that

70 *See,* S.Rep. No. 104-366, 104th Cong., 2d Sess. 37 (1996).

witnesses in federal courts "shall be paid an attendance fee of $40 per day for each day's attendance." Thus, if no contract or expert witness fee-shifting statute provides otherwise, a fee award to an expert witness may not exceed $40 per day; the only exception is "when the witness is court-appointed." *Id.* at 442.[71]

The Court based its opinion on its reading of 28 U.S.C. § 1821 together with 28 U.S.C. § 1920 and Federal Rule of Civil Procedure 54(d). It rejected the view that

> § 1920 does not preclude taxation of costs above and beyond the items listed, and more particularly, amounts in excess of the § 1821 fee. Thus, the discretion granted by Rule 54(d) is a separate source of power to tax as costs expenses not enumerated in § 1920. We think, however, that no reasonable reading of these provisions together can lead to this conclusion, for petitioners' view renders § 1920 superfluous. If Rule 54(d*)* grants courts discretion to tax whatever costs may seem appropriate, then § 1920, which enumerates the costs that may be taxed, serves no role whatsoever. We think the better view is that § 1920 defines the term "costs" as used in Rule 54(d). Section 1920 enumerates expenses that a federal court may tax as a cost under the discretionary authority found in Rule 54(d).

Id. at 441-442.

In *West Virginia University Hospitals, Inc. v. Casey,* 499 U.S. 83, 87 (1991), the Supreme Court held that "the term 'attorney's fee' in § 1988" does not provide "the 'explicit statutory authority' required by *Crawford Fitting"* for the shifting of expert fees.[72] The Civil Rights Act of 1991, Public Law 102-166, § 113, authorized courts to include expert fees as part of the attorney's fee under 42 U.S.C. § 1981 and 1981a, and under Title Vll of the Civil Rights Act of 1964,42 U.S.C. § 2000e-5(k). 42 U.S.C. § 1988(c).[73]

Awards of Costs For and Against the United States

At common law, the United States could recover costs "as if they were a private individual." *Pine River Logging Co. v. United States,* 186 U.S. 279, 296 (1902). No statute has changed this. Costs against the United States, however, at common law were barred by sovereign immunity, absent express statutory consent. *Id.* The provision of Rule 54(d) that "costs against the United States, its officers, and agencies shall be imposed only to the extent permitted by law," "is merely declaratory and

---

71 At the time of *Crawford Fitting,* witness fees were set at $30; Public Law 101-650, § 314, raised them to $40.

72 The Court listed "34 statutes in 10 different titles of the U.S. Code [that] explicitly shift attorney's fees *and* [emphasis supplied by the Court] expert witness fees." 499 U.S. at 89.

effected no change in principle." *Reconstruction Finance Corp. v. J.G. Menihan Corp.,* 312 U.S. 81, 83 (1941).

Costs were made allowable against the United States in 1966 by 28 U.S.C. § 2412(a). that provides:

> Except as otherwise specifically provided by statute a judgement for costs, as enumerated in section 1920 of this title but not including the fees and expenses of attorneys may be awarded to the prevailing party in any civil action brought by or against the United States....

A Senate report said that the 1966 change was enacted to correct the —

> disparity of treatment between private litigants and the United States concerning the allowance of court costs... . As things now stand, only in rare cases can costs be awarded against the United States in the event that it is the losing party. On the other hand when it sues on a claim and wins, it can collect full costs.[74]

Whether this disparity has been entirely eliminated appears questionable, because Rule 54(d), which allows costs against parties other than the United States, provides that costs "shall be allowed as of course," whereas § 2412, which allows costs against the United States, provides only that costs "may be awarded."

DETERMINING A REASONABLE ATTORNEYS' FEE

The amount of attorneys' fees to be awarded pursuant to a statutory or common law exception to the American rule "should, as a general rule, be fixed in the first instance by the District Court, after hearing evidence as to the extent and nature of the services rendered." *Perkins v. Standard Oil of California,* 399 U.S. 222, 223 (1970).

The evidence presented to the district court must be relatively specific:

> It is not necessary to know the exact number of minutes spent nor the precise activity to which each hour was devoted nor the specific attainment of each attorney. But without some fairly definite information as to the hours devoted to various general activities, e.g., pretrial discovery, settlement negotiations. and tire hours spent by various classes of attorneys, *e.g.,* senior partners, junior partners, associates, the court cannot know the nature of the services for which compensation is sought.

---

73 *See, Attorneys' Fees and Expert Witness Fees Under the Civil Rights Act of 1991* (CRS Report No. 91-818A, Nov. 20, 1991).

74 S.Rep. No. 1329, 89th Cong., 2d Sess. (1966); *reprinted in* 1966 U.S.C.C.A.N. 2527, 2528.

Lindv Bros. Builders, Inc. v. American Radiator & Standard Sanitary Corp., 487 F.2d 161, 167 (3d Cir. 1973).

In *Pennsylvania* v. *Delaware Valley Citizens' Council for Clean Air (Delaware Valley I),* 478 U.S. 546, 562-566 (1986), the Supreme Court explained "the proper measure for determining the 'reasonableness' of a particular fee award":

> One method, first employed by the Fifth Circuit in *Johnson v. Georgia Highway Express, Inc.*, 488 F .2d 714 (1974), involved consideration of 12 factors. *Johnson* was widely followed by other courts, and was cited with approval by both the House and the Senate when [42 U.S.C.] § 1988 was enacted....[75] Setting attorney's fees by reference to a series of sometimes subjective factors placed unlimited discretion in trial judges and produced disparate results.
>
> For this reason, the Third Circuit developed another method of calculating "reasonable" attorney's fees. This method, known as the "lodestar" approach, involved two steps. First, the court was to calculate the "lodestar," determined by multiplying the hours spent on a case by a reasonable hourly rate of compensation for each attorney involved. *Lindy Bros. Builders, Inc. v. American Radiator & Standard Sanitary Corp.*, 487 F. 2d 161, 167 (CA3 1973) (*Lindy I*). Second, using the lodestar figure as a starting point, the court could then make adjustments to this figure, in light of "(1) the contingent nature of the case, reflecting the likelihood that hours were invested and expenses incurred without assurance of compensation; and (2) the quality of the work performed as evidenced by the work observed, the complexity of the issues and the recovery obtained...."
>
> We first addressed the question of the proper manner in which to determine a "reasonable" attorney's fee in *Hensley v. Eckerhart,* 461 U.S. 424 (1983). We there adopted a hybrid approach that shared elements of both the *Johnson* and the lodestar method of calculation. "The most useful starting point for determining the amount of a reasonable fee is the number of hours reasonably expended on the litigation multiplied by a reasonable hourly rate...." To this extent, the method endorsed in *Hensley* follows the Third Circuit's description of the first step of the lodestar approach. Moreover, we went on to state: "The product of reasonable hours times a reasonable rate does not end the inquiry. There remain other considerations that may lead the district court to adjust the fee upward or downward.... We then took a more expansive view of what those "other considerations" might be, however, noting that

[75] Footnote 7 of the Court's opinion states: "The 12 factors are: (1) the time and labor required; (2) the novelty and difficulty of the question; (3) the skill requisite to perform the legal service properly; (4) the preclusion of other employment by the attorney due to acceptance of the case; (5) the customary fee; (6) whether the fee is fixed or contingent; (7) time limitations imposed by the client or the circumstances; (8) the amount involved and the results obtained; (9) the experience, reputation, and ability of attorney; (10) the "undesirability" of the case; (11) the nature and length of the professional relationship with the client; and (12) awards in similar cases. 488 F.2d, at 717-719, These factors were taken from the American Bar Association Code of Professional Responsibility, Disciplinary Rule 2-106 (1980)." They are now embodied in the American Bar Association Model Rules of Professional Conduct, Rule 1.5 (1983).

> "[the] factors identified in *Johnson v. Georgia Highway Express, Inc.*, 488 F. 2d 714, 717-719 (CA5 1974), though it should note that many of these factors usually are subsumed within the initial calculation of hours reasonably expended at a reasonable hourly rate." *Id.*, at 434, n. 9 (citation omitted).
>
> We further refined our views in *Blum v. Stenson* 465 U.S. 886 (1984).... *Blum* also limited the factors which a district court may consider in determining whether to make adjustments to the lodestar amount. Expending on our earlier finding in *Hensley* that many of the *Johnson* factors "are subsumed within the initial calculation" of the lodestar, we specifically held in *Blum* that the "novelty [and] complexity of the issues," "the special skill and competence of counsel," the "quality of representation," and the "result obtained from the litigation are presumably fully reflected in lodestar ... and thus cannot serve as independent bases for increasing the basic fee award. 465 U.S., at 898-900. Although upward adjustments of the lodestar figure are still permissible, *id.*, at 901, such modifications are proper only in certain "rare" and "exceptional" cases, supported by both "specific evidence" on the record and detailed findings by the lower courts.[76]
>
> In short, the lodestar figure includes most, if not all of the relevant factors comprising a "reasonable" attorney's fee, and it is unnecessary to enhance the fee for superior performance in order to serve the statutory purpose of enabling plaintiffs to secure legal assistance.[77]

In *Delaware Valley I,* the Court indicated that to be entitled to an upward adjustment, a prevailing party must show that it would have been unable "to obtain counsel without any promise of reward for extraordinary performance." It must present "specific evidence as to what made the results it obtained... so 'outstanding.'" It must show "that the lodestar figure… was far below awards made in similar cases where the court found equally superior quality of performance." Finally, to adjust a fee upward, a court must make "detailed findings as to why the lodestar amount was unreasonable, and in particular as to why the quality of representation was not reflected in the number of hours times the reasonable hourly rate." 478 U.S. at 567-568. The Court left open "the question of upward adjustment based on the likelihood of success, or to put it another way, the risk of loss." *Id.* at 568. By "risk of loss" the Court apparently meant an attorney's risk of losing and not being paid at all because he had agreed to represent his client on a contingency basis, being paid out of the winnings or not at all.

The Court answered this question in a second opinion in the same case. *Pennsylvania v. Delaware Valley Citizens' Council for Clean Air (Delaware Valley*

---

76 Upward adjustments are also called "bonuses." The Supreme Court has stated that it thinks the characterization "upward adjustments" is "fairer." Blum v. Stenson, 465 U.S. at 896 n.12. Upward adjustments may be made "by way of multipliers or enhancement of the lodestar." *Delaware Valley I,* 478 U.S. at 568.

77 The dissent thought that the Court had "improperly heightened the showing required to the point where it may be virtually impossible for a plaintiff to meet." 478 U.S. at 569.

II,), 483 U.S. 711 (1987), which was a 4-1-4 decision. Justice O'Connor concurred in parts of each plurality, which makes her opinion pivotal in determining what a majority of the Court decided in the case. Five justices (Justice O'Connor and the four who joined Justice Blackmun's dissent) decided that upward adjustments generally are appropriate in contingency fee cases. However, five justices (Justice O'Connor and the four who joined Justice White's plurality), decided that, even if "typical fee-shifting statutes are construed to permit supplementing the lodestar in appropriate cases by paying counsel for assuming the risk of nonpayment... it was error to do so in this case." 483 U.S. at 728.

Subsequently, however, in *Burlington v. Dague,* 505 U.S. 557, 567 (1992), the Court, "[a]dopting the position set forth in Justice White's opinion in *Delaware Valley II*" held "that enhancement for contingency is not permitted under the fee-shifting statutes at issue." Those statutes were § 7002(e) of the Solid Waste Disposal Act, 42 U.S.C. § 6972(e), and § 505(d) of the Clean Water Act, 33 U.S.C. § 1365(d). However, the Court noted that the relevant language of these statutes "is similar to that of many other federal fee-shifting statutes...; our case law construing what is a 'reasonable' fee applies uniformly to all of them." *Id.* at 562. The Court's primary reason for its decision in *Burlington* was "that an enhancement for contingency would likely duplicate in substantial part factors already subsumed in the lodestar." *Id.*

In *Blum v. Stenson, 465* U.S. 886, 895 (1984), the Supreme Court held that "'reasonable fees' are to be calculated under [42 U.S.C.] § 1988 according to the prevailing market rates in the relevant community, regardless of whether the plaintiff is represented by private or nonprofit counsel."[78] The Court rejected the position that awards be calculated according to the cost of providing legal services, which for legal aid groups that pay low salaries is usually less than the prevailing market rates.[79]

The Handicapped Children's Protection Act of 1986, Public Law 99-372, which added an attorneys' fees provision to the Education of the Handicapped Act, adopted

---

78 In *Blum v. Stenson,* the Court also contrasted calculation of fee awards under the common fund doctrine (see pp. 2-3 of this report) and under § 1988. Under the former "a reasonable fee is based on a percentage of the fund bestowed on the class," while "a reasonable fee under § 1988 reflects the amount of attorney time reasonably expended on the litigation." 465 U.S. at 900 n.16. Risk multipliers are also more permissible in common fund cases. *See, e.g.,* Florin v. Nationsbank of Georgia, 34 F.3d 560 (7th Cir. 1994); *In re* Washington Public Power Supply System Securities Litigation, 19 F.3d 1291 (9th Cir. 1994); Swedish Hospital Corp. v. Shalala, 1 F.3d 1261 (D.C. Cir. 1993); Camden I Condominium Association v. Dunkle., 946 F.2d 768 (11 Cir. 1991); Skelton v. General Motors Corp., 860 F.2d 250 (7th Cir. 1988).

79 Funds received from the Legal Services Corporation may not be used to provide legal assistance with respect to fee-generating cases, with some exceptions. 42 U.S.C. § 2996f(b)(l). A "fee-generating" case includes any case that "reasonably may be expected to result in a fee for legal services from an award to a client, from public funds, or from the opposing party." 45 C.F.R. § 1609.2. Public Law 104-134, § 504, provides: "None of the funds appropriated in this Act to the Legal Services Corporation may be used to provide financial assistance to any person or entity...(13) that claims (or whose employee claims), or collects and retains, attorneys' fees pursuant to any Federal or State law permitting or requiting the awarding of such fees...."

this feature of *Blum v. Stenson,* but at the same time prohibited upward adjustments entirely. The statute, 20 U.S.C. § 1415(e)(4)(C), provides:

> For purposes of this subsection, fees awarded under this subsection shall be based on rates prevailing in the community in which the action or proceeding arose for the kind and quality of services furnished. No bonus or multiplier may be used in calculating fees awarded under this subsection.

In *Laffey v. Northwest Airlines, Inc.,* 746 F.2d4 (D.C. Cir. 1984), *cert. denied,* 472 U.S. 1021 (1985), the court of appeals held that, for purposes of computing awards of attorneys' fees in civil rights cases, although a nonprofit legal organization is entitled under *Blum v. Stenson* to the prevailing market rate, a "for-profit" law firm that ordinarily charges less than the prevailing market rate — a" 'quasi' public interest law firm," as the court called it in footnote 69 — is entitled "in almost every case" only to its "established billing rates." *id.* at 24. In *Save Our Cumberland Mountains, Inc. v. Hodel,* 857 F.2d 1516, 1520 (D.C. Cir. 1988) (en banc), the full court of appeals overruled *Laffey,* on the ground that its "anomalous" result was not intended by Congress. "Henceforth," the court wrote, "the prevailing market rate method heretofore used in awarding fees to traditional for-profit firms and public interest firms and public interest legal service organizations shall apply as well to those attorneys who practice privately and for profit but at reduced rates reflecting non--economic goals." *Id.* at 1524.

In *City of Riverside v. Rivera,* 477 U.S. 561, 564 (1986), the Supreme Court held that, under 42 U.S.C. § 1988(b), an award of attorneys' fees is not "per se 'unreasonable' within the meaning of the statute if it exceeds the amount of damages recovered by the plaintiff in the underlying civil rights action." The Court wrote:

> Unlike most private tort litigants, a civil rights plaintiff seeks to vindicate important civil and constitutional rights that cannot be valued solely in monetary terms... . And, Congress has determined that "the public as a whole has an interest in the vindication of the rights conferred by the statutes enumerated in § 1988, over and above the value of a civil rights remedy to a particular plaintiff...."

Id. at 574.

Nevertheless, in *Farrar v. Hobby,* 506 U.S. 103, 115 (1992), the Supreme Court held that, under 42 U.S.C. § 1988(b), "[w]hen a plaintiff recovers only nominal damages because of his failure to prove an essential element of his claim for monetary relief... , the only reasonable fee is usually no fee at all." The Court held that a plaintiff who is awarded only nominal damages — in this case one dollar when he had sought $17 million — is a prevailing party for attorneys' fees purposes, as he had established "the violation of his right to procedural due process." *Id.* at 112. However, because he could not prove actual injury, lie was not entitled to a fee a ward.

What if a prevailing party is entitled to an award of "reasonable" fees from his opponent and has also agreed to pay his lawyer a contingent fee? Under 42 U.S.C.§ 1988(b), if the "reasonable" fee is higher, then, the Supreme Court held in *Blanchard v. Bergeron,* 489 U.S. 87 (1989), the defendant must pay the higher fee. If the contingent fee is higher, then. the Supreme Court held in *Venegas v Mitchel,* 495 U.S. 82 (1990),. the defendant is liable only for the "reasonable" fee, but the plaintiff must still pay his lawyer the higher contingent fee. The Court emphasized in *Venegas* that "Section 1988 makes the prevailing *party* eligible for a discretionary award of attorney's fees." *Id.* at 87 (emphasis supplied by the Court). It would seem to follow that, in the *Blanchard* situation, where the "reasonable" fee is higher, the prevailing party may keep the difference between the "reasonable" fee paid by the defendant and the amount owed under the contingent fee agreement. This inference is supported by the Court's statement in *Venegas* that it "rejected the argument that the entitlement to a § 1988 award belongs to the attorney rather than the plaintiff." *Id.* at 89. Yet, in *Blanchard,* the Court wrote:

> Respondent cautions us that refusing to limit recovery to the amount of the contingency agreement will result in a "windfall" to *attorneys* who accept § 1983 actions. Yet the very nature of recovery under § 1988 is designed to prevent any such "windfall." Fee awards are to be reasonable....

489 U.S. at 96 (emphasis added).[80]

In *Missouri v. Jenkins,* 491 U.S. 274 (1989), in addition to deciding the Eleventh Amendment question discussed in section IX of this report, the Supreme Court held that, under § 1988(b), the time of paralegals and law clerks should be considered in determining the amount of a fee award.

Finally, there is the question of how to compute fee awards against the United States. Under the Equal Access to Justice Act and under the Internal Revenue Code, awards ordinarily are limited to $125 per hour. Apart from this, fee awards against the United States are calculated the same way as fee awards against other parties. *Copeland v. Marshall,* 641 F.2d 880 (D.C. Cit. 1980) *(en bane).* The full court of appeals in this case reversed an earlier opinion by a three judge panel of the court. 594 F.2d 244 (D.C. Cir. 1978). The panel had held that the *Johnson* guidelines:

> are applicable generally to Title Vii cases against a federal agency, but that special caution must be shown by the trial court in scrutinizing the claims of attorneys for fees against a federal agency in such litigation. Special caution is required be cause of the incentive which the defendant's "deep pocket" offers to attorneys to inflate their

---

80 *See*, Annotation, *Effect of Contingent Fee Contract on Fee Award Authorized by Federal Statute,* 76 ALR Fed 347.

> billing charges and to claim far more as reimbursement than would be sought or could reasonably be recovered from most private parties.

Id. at 250. To exercise that caution, the court wrote:

> The trial court should give consideration to abandoning the traditional claimed hourly-fee starting point for its calculations in favor of a principle of reimbursement to a firm for its costs, plus a reasonable and controllable margin for profit.

Id. at 251.

This "cost-plus" formula would have lowered fee awards in Title VII cases against the federal government, and consequently had been called "a serious blow to the whole public interest law movement." *(N.Y. Times,* Nov. 14, 1978, at A25). The three judge panel, however, on June 29, 1979, denied a rehearing and issued an unreported opinion clarifying its decision.

The full court of appeals reversed, writing that it did "not think that the amount of the fee should depend on the identity of the losing party." 641 F.2d at 894. It noted that Title VII provides that the United States shall be liable for costs the same as a private person," and that the incentive supplied by fee awards to refrain from discrimination should not be less for the government than it is for private employers. *Id.* at 895. Furthermore, the court feared "that the proposed 'cost-plus' method of calculating fees would indeed become the inquiry of 'massive proportions' that we strive to avoid." *Id.* at 896. In sum, the court believed that in Title VII cases, against the government or otherwise, attorneys should be compensated "for the market value of the services rendered." *Id.* at 900.

RULE 68 OF THE FEDERAL RULES OF CIVIL PROCEDURE

Rule 68 of the Federal Rules of Civil Procedure, 28 U.S.C. App. Rule 68, creates an exception to the general rule in federal courts that a prevailing party is entitled to collect its court costs from the losing party. "The plain purpose of Rule 68 is to encourage settlement and avoid litigation." *Marek v. Chesny,* 473 U.S. 1, 5 (1985). Rule 68 provides that if, at any time more than 10 days before a trial begins, a party defending against a claim offers a settlement including costs then accrued,[81] and the offeree fails to accept the offer within 10 days, then, if the offeree wins the lawsuit, but the judgment he obtains "is not more favorable than the offer, the offeree must pay

[81] An offer under Rule 68 need not "separately recite the amount that the defendant is offering in settlement of the substantive claim and the amount he is offering to cover accrued costs... As long as the offer does not implicitly or explicitly provide that the judgment not include costs, a timely offer will be valid." Marek v. Chesny. 473 U.S. 1, 5, 6 (1985).

the costs incurred after the making of the offer."[82] In other words, the plaintiff forfeits his right under Rule 54(d) to recover costs incurred after such time.[83]

In *Marek v. Chesny,* the Supreme Court addressed the interaction of Rule 68 and the Civil Rights Attorney's Fees Awards Act of 1976, 42 U.S.C. § 1988(b). Section 1988(b) authorizes the award of "a reasonable attorney's fee as part of the costs" in suits brought under 42 U.S.C. § 1983, and several other civil rights statutes. The Court held that, if a lawsuit is brought under a statute, such as § 1988(b), that provides for awards of attorneys' fees as *part* of the costs, then the term "costs" in Rule 68 includes attorneys' fees. The Court viewed this as the " 'plain meaning' interpretation of the interplay between Rule 68 and § 1988." *Id.* at 9.

This decision means that Rule 68 creates an exception not only to Rule 54(d*),* but also to all statutes that authorize awards of attorneys' fees to prevailing parties as part of the costs. Under *Marek v. Chesny,* a prevailing plaintiff otherwise entitled to recover attorneys' fees under one of these statutes is not entitled to recover attorneys' fees incurred after an offer to settle was made if the prevailing plaintiff rejected the offer and then won no more than had been offered.[84]

The dissent in *Marek v. Chesny* pointed out that this means that "Rule 68 will operate to *include* the potential loss of otherwise-recoverable attorney's fees as an incentive to settlement in litigation under" the following statutes (of which the dissent listed 63): those that refer "to the awarding of 'attorney's fees *as part of* the costs,' to 'costs *including* attorney's fees,' and to 'attorney's fees and *other* litigation costs."' *Id.* at 23. Rule 68 will *not* include the potential loss of attorneys' fees in statutes (of which the dissent listed 49) that refer "to the awarding of 'costs *and* a reasonable attorney's fee,' of 'costs *together* with a reasonable attorney's fee,' or simply of 'attorney's fees' without reference to costs." *Id.* In addition, as the dissent pointed out: "A number of statutes authorize the award of 'costs and expenses, including attorney's fees.' It is altogether uncertain how such statutes [of which the dissent listed 7] should be categorized under the Court's 'plain language' approach to Rule 68" *Id.* at 44. In short, the dissent believed that *Marek v. Chesny* sanctions "a senseless patchwork of

---

82 Rule 68 also provides that the fact that an offer is not accepted does not preclude a subsequent offer, and that, if a party is adjudged liable for a claim, but the amount of liability remains to be determined, the party adjudged liable may then offer to settle, and the offer shall have the same effect as an offer made before trial.

83 However, according to *Grossman v. Marcoccio,* 806 F.2d 329, 332 (5th Cir. 1986), *cert. denied,* 481 U.S. 1029 (1987), Rule 68 not only alters the Rule 54(d) presumption in favor of the prevailing party's recovering its own costs, it "obligates plaintiffs to pay defendants' post-offer costs after rejecting an offer more favorable than the judgment eventually obtained." *Accord,* O'Brien v. City of Greers Ferry, 873 F.2d 1115 (8th Cir. 1989).

84 The prevailing plaintiff never, however, has to pay the defendant's post-offer attorneys' fees, even under the two cases cited in the previous footnote. As these cases noted, this is because a civil rights defendant may not be awarded attorneys' fees unless he prevails (which, under the these cases, he need not do to recover costs under Rule 68) and unless the court determines that the plaintiffs action was "frivolous, unreasonable, or without foundation" (which it would not be in a case in which the plaintiff prevails).

fee-shifting that flies in the face of the fundamental purpose of the Federal Rules — the provision of uniform and consistent procedure in federal courts." *Id.* at 24.

If Congress wishes to restore uniformity with respect to the effect of Rule 68 on awards of attorneys' fees, then it could amend Rule 68 to define "costs" as used in Rule 68 either to include or to exclude attorneys' fees in suits brought under statutes authorizing awards of attorneys' fees. If it defines "costs" to include attorneys' fees, then attorneys' fees incurred after an offer would not be recoverable by plaintiffs who reject a settlement offer and then fail to win more than they had been offered. If it defines "costs" to exclude attorneys' fees, then such parties would lose their opportunity under Rule 54(d) to be awarded costs incurred after an offer, but would retain their entitlement to an award of attorneys' fees.

Alternatively, Congress could amend individual attorneys' fees statutes to provide that attorneys' fees may be awarded either as part of the costs or in addition to costs. It will also have to make this decision with respect to attorneys' fees statutes it enacts in the future.[85] In the Handicapped Children's Protection Act of 1986, Public Law 99-372, which was enacted after *Marek v. Chesny,* Congress adopted a compromise approach to settlement offers. It included a provision modeled on Rule 68 that bars recovery of attorney's fees and costs of plaintiffs who reject settlement offers, and applies to administrative proceedings as well as to civil actions under the Individuals with Disabilities Education Act (formerly the Education of the Handicapped Act; *see,* pp. 31-32, *supra).* However, it allows a prevailing plaintiff who would otherwise forfeit costs and attorneys' fees to recover them nevertheless if he had been substantially justified in rejecting a settlement offer. 20 U.S.C. § 1415(e)(4)(D). The conference report that accompanied the legislation stated: "Substantial justification for rejection would include relevant pending court decisions that could have an impact on the case in question."[86]

NEGOTIATED FEE WAIVERS

In *Evans v. Jeff D.,* 475 U.S. 717(1986), the Supreme Court upheld the legality of negotiated waivers of attorneys' fees. *Evans* was a class action brought under 42 U.S.C. § 1983 seeking injunctive relief concerning the conditions of mentally and emotionally handicapped children institutionalized by the State of Idaho. One week before trial, the defendant offered the plaintiffs virtually all the injunctive relief they had sought — on condition that the plaintiffs waive their claim to fees and costs under

85 The Civil Rights Act of 1990, S. 2104, 101st Congress, which was vetoed by President Bush, would have amended Title VII of the Civil Rights Act of 1964, 42 U.S.C. § 2000e-5(k), to authorize "a reasonable attorney's fee... and costs," instead of "a reasonable attorney's fee as part of the costs," as it now reads.

86 H.Rept. 99-687, 99th Cong., 2d Sess. 6 (1986), *reprinted in* 1986 U.S.C.C.A.N. 1807, 1809.

42 U.S.C. § 1988(b). The plaintiffs lawyer "determined that his ethical obligation to his clients mandated acceptance of the proposal" (*Id.* at 722),[87] but he requested the district court to approve the settlement except for the provision on costs and attorneys' fees. (Class action settlements must be approved by the court under Rule 23 of the Federal Rules of Civil Procedure.) The district court upheld the fee waiver, but the court of appeals reversed on the ground that § 1988(b) "normally requires an award of fees to prevailing plaintiffs in civil rights actions, including those who have prevailed through settlement. The court added that '[w]hen attorney's fees are negotiated as part of a class action settlement, a conflict of interest frequently exists between the class lawyers' interest in compensation and the class members' interest in relief'" *Id.* at 725. If negotiated fee waivers are permitted, then a defendant can exploit a plaintiffs lawyer's ethical obligation to his client to force him to waive fees that Congress arguably intended him to recover.

The Supreme Court rejected this view, holding that "[t]he statute and its legislative history nowhere suggest that Congress intended to forbid *all* waivers of attorney's fees...." *Id.* at 731. The Court added that "there are many... civil rights actions in which potential liability for attorney's fees may overshadow the potential cost of relief on the merits and darken prospects for settlement if fees cannot be negotiated." *Id.* at. 735.

In response to these two points of the majority, the dissent argued first, that, although there is no evidence that Congress intended to ban all fee waivers, "[t]here is no evidence that Congress gave the question of fee waivers any thought at all" *(Id.* at 743-744), and second, that *"a judicial* policy favoring settlements cannot possibly take precedence over... express *congressional* policy" favoring "incentives for lawyers to devote time to civil rights cases" *(Id.* at 760-761). The dissent concluded:

> Although today's decision will undoubtedly impair the effectiveness of the private enforcement scheme Congress established for civil rights legislation, I do not believe that it will bring about the total disappearance of "private attorneys general." It is to be hoped that Congress will repair this Court's mistake. In the meantime, other avenues of relief are available.... Indeed, several Bar Associations have already declared it unethical for defense counsel to seek fee waivers.... In addition, it may be that civil rights attorneys can obtain agreements from their clients not to waive attorney's fees.

Id. at 765-766.[88]

---

87 The Supreme Court wrote: "it is argued that an attorney is required to evaluate a settlement offer on the basis of his client's interest, without considering his own interest in obtaining a fee; upon recommending settlement, he must abide by the client's decision whether or not to accept the offer." *Id.* at 728 n.14. The Court stated that the plaintiffs' lawyer's decision in this case "to recommend acceptance was consistent with the highest standards of our profession." *Id.* at 728.

88 The majority and the dissent agreed that § 1988(b) "should not be interpreted to prohibit simultaneous negotiations of a defendant's liability on the merits and his liability for his opponent's attorney's

STATUTORY LIMITATIONS ON ATTORNEYS' FEES

Some federal statutes and regulations limit the amount attorneys may charge their clients for representing them before various federal agencies. These provisions have different types of limitations. For example, 38 U.S.C. § 5904(d) limits contingent fees in cases before the Department of Veterans Affairs to 20 percent of past-due benefits awarded; 15 U.S.C. §§ 79g(d)(4) and 79j(b)(2)) provide that the amount of compensation paid under the Public Utility Holding Company Act of 1935 is subject to approval of the Securities and Exchange Commission; and 42 U.S.C. § 1383(d)(2) provides that the Secretary of Health and Human Services shall by rule and regulation prescribe maximum fees in Supplemental Security Income cases.[89]

Some of these attorneys' fees limitations are controversial because, although they may protect claimants from having to pay to their attorneys a large portion of any amount awarded, they may also so limit fees as to deter lawyers from handling cases, thus in effect denying claimants legal representation. The Supreme Court, however, held that the former $10 ceiling in Veterans' Administration cases is not unconstitutional for this reason. *Walters v. National Association of Radiation Survivors,* 473 U.S. 305 (1985). The Court noted Congress's desire "that the system should be as informal and non-adversarial as possible." *Id.* at 323-324. The Court did not, however, preclude the possibility that the $10 limitation could be unconstitutional as applied in a particular case. *See, id.* at 336 (O'Connor, J., concurring).

In *United States Department of Labor v. Triplett,* 494 U.S. 715 (1990), the Supreme Court upheld the fee limitations of the Black Lung Benefits Act. 30, U.S.C. § 932(a). which are incorporated from the Longshore and Harbor Workers' Compensation Act, 33 U. S.C. § 928. These limitations prohibit an attorney from receiving a fee unless approved by the appropriate agency or court. In addition, "[t]he Department's regulations invalidate all contractual arrangements for fees... and the Department will not approve a fee if the claimant is unsuccessful." *Id.* at 718. The Court concluded that there was no evidence adequate to "establish *either* that black lung claimants are unable to retain qualified counsel *or* that the cause of such inability is the attorney's fee system administered by the Department." *Id.* at 726 (emphasis in original). Therefore, there was "no basis for concluding that that system deprives claimants of property without due process of law." *Id.*

The American Bar Association's Special Committee on Federal Limitations on Attorneys' Fees recommended in August, 1980 that Congress enact legislation

---

fees." *Id.* at 738 n.3 0. The dissent, however, would have permitted the parties to negotiate "reasonable" fees, not waivers. *Id.* at 764-765.

89 A summary of federal statutes and regulations that limit attorneys' fees is published in Robert L. Rossi, ATTORNEYS' FEES (2d ed.) § 2.10 (Lawyers Co-operative Pub. Co., 1995). Public Law 104-201, § 657(i), imposed a 10 percent ceiling on attorneys' fees for representing a person claiming compensation for being a prisoner of war in Vietnam.

establishing uniform principles for the regulation of attorneys' fees in proceedings conducted before federal administrative agencies, and that such legislation prohibit arbitrary maximum fees and provide for reasonable fees.

Funding of Participants in Federal Agency Proceedings

Federal agencies, like federal courts, may not, absent statutory authority, order one party to a proceeding to pay the attorneys' fees of another. Even the common law exceptions to the American rule are unavailable to federal agencies, as those exceptions stem from the inherent power of federal courts to do equity. *Turner v. Federal Communications Commission,* 514 F.2d 1354 (D.C. Cir. 1975). In addition, courts of appeals for two circuits have held that, absent statutory authority, an agency may not pay the attorneys' fees of participants in its proceedings. *Greene County Planning Board v. Federal Power Commission*, 559 F.2d 1227 (2d Cir. 1976), *rev'd on rehearing en banc, 559* F.2dat 1237, cert. *denied,* 434 U.S. 1086 (1 978); *Pacific Legal Foundation v. Goyan,* 664 F.2d 1221 (4th Cir. 1981).[90]

Three federal agencies have explicit statutory authority to provide compensation for reasonable attorneys' fees, expert witness fees, and other costs of participating in their proceedings: the Environmental Protection Agency, which has such authority for rulemaking proceedings under the Toxic Substances Control Act (15 U.S.C. § 2605(c)(4)), the Federal Energy Regulatory Commission, which has such authority for all proceedings before it (16 U.S.C. § 825q-1 (b)(2)), and the Department of State, which has such authority for all proceedings, advisory committees, and delegations (22 U.S.C. § 2692).[91] In addition, the Consumer Product Safety Commission may contribute to any person's cost with respect to participation with the Commission in the development of a consumer product safety standard (15 U.S.C. § 2056(c)).

Notwithstanding these statutes, Congress has refused to allow EPA or FERC to compensate participants in their proceedings. Public Law 103-327 (1994), § 510, which appropriated funds for EPA, provides:

> None of the funds in this Act shall be used to pay the expenses of, or otherwise compensate, non-Federal parties intervening in regulatory or adjudicatory proceedings. Nothing herein affects the authority of the Consumer Product Safety

90 *See,* Annotation, *Authority of Federal Agency to Spend Public Funds to Reimburse Expenses of Qualified Participants in its Proceedings,* 62 ALR Fed 849.

91 The Federal Trade Commission formerly had such authority for all its rulemaking proceedings. P.L, 93-637 (1975), § 202(a);formerly codified at 15 U.S.C. § 57a(h); repealed by P.L. 103-312 (1994), § 3.

Commission pursuant to section 7 of the Consumer Product Safety Act (15 U.S.C. 2056 et seq.).

Public Law 102-377 (1992), § 502, which appropriated funds for FERC, provides:

> "None of the funds in this Act or subsequent Energy and Water Development Appropriations Acts shall be used to pay the expenses of, or otherwise compensate, parties intervening in regulatory or adjudicatory proceedings funded in such Acts."[92]

At one time, several federal agencies without explicit statutory authority to fund intervenors did so under what they viewed as their general statutory powers, and had the support of the Comptroller General in so doing. The latter, in a decision (B-92288), wrote:

> [I]f the NRC in the exercise of its administrative discretion, determines that it cannot make the required determination unless it extends financial assistance to certain interested parties who require it, and whose participation is essential to dispose of the matter before it, we would not object to the use of appropriated funds for this purpose.[93]

The courts, however, decided the *Greene County* and *Pacific Legal Foundation* cases cited above, and Congress eliminated most intervenor funding by prohibiting it in appropriations measures, such as those cited above.

Some Arguments For and Against the American Rule

One line of arguments for and against the American rule centers around the philosophical question of whose expense an attorney should be. "in support of the American rule it has been argued that since litigation is at best uncertain, one should not be penalized for merely defending or prosecuting a lawsuit...." *Fleisclzmann v. Maier Brewing Co.,* 386 U.S. 714. 718 (1967). "[T]he expenses of litigation are… not the 'natural and proximate consequences of the wrongful act'… but are remote, future

92 Congress apparently has placed no similar restriction on the Department of State, but an attorney at the Department of State informed us that it has not used its authority to fund intervenors in recent years and may never have done so.

93 In a subsequent letter (B-180224), the Comptroller General indicated that the above decision applied to several other agencies. This letter appears in a committee print of the Senate Committee on Commerce entitled Agency Comments on the Payment of Reasonable Fees for Public Participation in Agency Proceedings, 95th Cong., 1st Sess. (1977). *See also,* B-139703 and 56 C.G. 111 (1976).

and contingent." *St. Peter's Church v. Beach,* 26 Conn. 355, 366 (1857). On the other hand, it has been noted that an injured person will not he made whole if he has to bear the expense of a lawyer. "[A] person who is successful in litigation is a part loser because he has to pay his own expenses and counsel fees, except a few minor items that are taxable as costs." *Rodulfa v. United States,* 295 F. Supp. 28 (D.D.C. 1969), *appeal dismissed,* 461 F.2d 1240 (D.C. Cir. 1972), *cert. denied,* 409 U.S. 949 (1972). "on what principle of justice can a plaintiff wrongfully rundown on a public highway recover his doctor's but not his lawyer's bill?" Judicial Council of Massachusetts, *First Report,* 11 Massachusetts Law Quarterly 1, 64 (1925).

Another line of arguments centers around the question of whether keeping or abandoning the American rule will more effectively further the public policy of encouraging meritorious claims and deterring non-meritorious ones. "Current practice tends to deter prosecution of even clearly meritorious claims by litigants who could at best recover less than the often high expenses of counsel.... And what is true for plaintiffs also holds true for defendants: the cost of defending against an unjust small claim may easily exceed the cost of simply paying what is demanded. The result is distasteful, for it ranks legal rights by dollar value...." *Court Awarded Attorney's Fees and Equal Access to the Courts,* 122 University of Pennsylvania Law Review 636, 650 (1974).

Requiring the loser to pay the winner's attorneys' fees might encourage litigation of some meritorious claims and discourage litigation of some nonmeritorious ones. On the other hand, the uncertainty of litigation might also lead to the opposite results. "[T]he poor might be unjustly discouraged from instituting actions to vindicate their rights if the penalty for losing included the fees of their opponents' counsel." *Fleischmann, supra.* In addition, non-meritorious claims might be encouraged by the prospect of avoiding the expense of a lawyer. However, it has also been argued in support of requiring losers to pay winners' lawyers' fees that, while conceding the uncertainty of litigation, it should be assumed that courts will more often than not arrive at a correct result. Otherwise, courts might as well be dispensed with entirely, as it would be cheaper and less time consuming simply to flip a coin.

In support of the American rule it has also been argued that "the time, expense, and difficulties of proof inherent in litigating the question of what constitutes reasonable attorney's fees would pose substantial burdens for judicial administration." *Fieischmann supra.* Since this comment was made, however, Congress has enacted many fee-shifting statutes that require courts to determine what constitutes a reasonable fee.

It has also been argued that abandonment of the American rule might have serious consequences for developing areas of the law, since potential litigants might be loath to espouse novel legal theories for fear of incurring additional expenses if they do not prevail.

Finally, since the prospect of an award of attorneys' fees might at times encourage suits and at other times deter them, the crowding of court calendars has been cited as an argument both for and against the American rule.

AWARDS OF ATTORNEYS' FEES TO PREVAILING CRIMINAL DEFENDANTS

Until the enactment of Public Law 105-119 in 1997, no federal statutory or common law exceptions to the American rule authorized fee-shifting from the losing to the winning party in federal criminal cases.[94] Of course, the Supreme Court has held that the Constitution requires the government to provide for the legal representation of indigent criminal defendants.[95] Congress does so with respect to persons accused of federal crimes in the Criminal Justice Act, 18 U.S.C. § 3006A.

Public Law 105-119, § 617, codified at 18 U.S.C. § 3006A note, provides, in pertinent part:

> the [federal] court, in any criminal case (other than a case in which the defendant is represented by assigned counsel paid for by the public)... may award to a prevailing party, other than the United States, a reasonable attorney's fee and other litigation expenses, where the court finds that the position of the United States was vexatious, frivolous, or in bad faith, unless the court finds that special circumstances make an award unjust. Such awards shall be granted pursuant to the procedures and limitations but not the burden of proof) provided for an award under section 2412 of title 28, United States Code....

Section 2412 is the Equal Access to Justice Act, and the procedures and limitations referred to are presumably those mentioned in § 2412(d), including the $125 per hour cap, and the ineligibility for fee awards of prevailing parties whose assets exceed the amounts specified. (These are spelled out at pp. 8-11, *supra*.) The burden of proof under EAJA is on the United States to prove that its position was substantially justified; the burden of proof under Public Law 105-119 is on the prevailing defendant to prove that the position of the United States was vexatious, frivolous, or in bad faith.

---

94 *See,* United States v. Horn, 29 F.3d 754 (1st Cir. 1994); *see also,* K.S. Rosenn, *Compensating the Innocent Accused,* 37 Ohio State L.J. 705 (1976). The Independent Counsel Reauthorization Act of 1987, 28 U.S.C. § 593 (f)(1), however, authorizes fee awards to investigated individuals who are not indicted.

95 Johnson v. Zerbst, 304 U.S. 458 (1938) (federal cases); Gideon v. Wainwright, 372 U.S. 355 (1963) (state cases).

Public Law 105-119 does not define "prevailing party," so the courts will have to determine whether it includes, for example, a defendant against whom charges are dropped prior to trial a defendant who is convicted of a lesser charge than the one brought, or a defendant whose conviction is reversed on appeal.

FEDERAL STATUTES THAT AUTHORIZE AWARDS OF ATTORNEYS' FEES

Ethics in Government Act of 1978

2 U.S.C. § 288i(d) *(see also,* 28 U.S.C. § 593(f))

"The Senate may by resolution authorize the reimbursement of any Member, officer, or employee of the Senate who is not represented by the [Senate Legal] Counsel for fees and costs, including attorneys' fees, reasonably incurred in obtaining representation. Such reimbursement shall be from funds appropriated to the contingent fund of the Senate."

Federal Contested Elections Act

2 U.S.C. § 396

"The committee [on House Administration of the House of Representatives] may allow any party reimbursement from the contingent fund of the House of Representatives of his reasonable expenses of the contested election case, including reasonable attorneys fees....

Government Employee Rights Act of 1991

2 U.S.C. § 1220(e)

"If the individual referred to in subsection (a) is the prevailing party in a proceeding under this section, attorney's fees maybe allowed by the court in accordance with the standards prescribed under section 706(k) of the Civil Rights Act of 1964 (42 U.S.C. 2000e-5(k))."

Congressional Accountability Act of 1995

2 U.S.C. § 1361(a)

"If a covered employee, with respect to any claim under this chapter, or a qualified person with a disability, with respect to any claim under section 1331 of this title, is a prevailing party in any proceeding under section 1405, 1406. 1407, or 1408 of this title, the hearing officer, Board, or court, as the case may be, may award attorney's fees, expert fees, and any other costs as would be appropriate if awarded under section 2005e-5(k) of Title 42."

Presidential and Executive Office Accountability Act

3 U.S.C. § 435(a) *(see also,* 28 U.S.C. § 3 905(a))

"If a covered employee, with respect to any claim under this chapter, or a qualified person with a disability, with respect to any claim under section 421 [making sections of the Americans with Disabilities Act of 1990 applicable to the White House and specified other executive facilities], is a prevailing party in any proceeding under section 453(1), the administrative agency may award attorney's fees, expert fees, and other costs as would be appropriate if awarded under section 706(k) of the Civil Rights Act of 1964."

Equal Access to Justice Act

5 U.S.C. § 504(a)(1) *(see also,* 28 U.S.C. § 2412)

"An agency that conducts an adversary adjudication shall award, to the prevailing party other than the United States, fees and other expenses incurred by that party in connection with that proceeding, unless the adjudicative officer of the agency finds that the position of the agency was substantially justified or that special circumstances make an award unjust."

Freedom of Information Act

5 U.S.C. § 552(a)(4)(E)

"The court may assess against the United States reasonable attorney fees and other litigation costs reasonably incurred in any case under this paragraph in which the complainant has substantially prevailed."

Privacy Act

5 U.S.C. § 552a(g)(2)(B)

"The court may assess against the United States reasonable attorney fees and other litigation costs reasonably incurred in any case under this paragraph in which the complainant has substantially prevailed."

5 U.S.C. § 552a(g)(3)(B)

"The court may assess against the United States reasonable attorney fees and other litigation costs reasonably incurred in any case under this paragraph in which the complainant has substantially prevailed."

5 U.S.C. § 552a(g)(4)

"In any suit brought under the provisions of subsection (g)(l)(C) or (D) of this section in which the court determines that the agency acted in a manner which was intentional or willful, the United States shall be liable to the individual in an amount equal to the sum of… the costs of the action together with reasonable attorney fees as determined by the court."

Government in the Sunshine Act

5 U.S.C. § 552b(i)

"The court may assess against any party reasonable attorney fees and other litigation costs reasonably incurred by any other party who substantially prevails in any action brought in accordance with the provisions of subsection (g) or (h) of this section, except that costs may be assessed against the plaintiff only where the court finds that the suit was initiated by the plaintiff primarily for frivolous or dilatory purposes. In the case of assessment of costs against an agency, the costs mar ha assessed by the court against the United States."

Whistleblower Protection Act of 1989

5 U.S.C. § 1204(m)(1)

"[T]he Board, or an administrative law judge or other employee of the Board designated to hear a case arising under section 1215, may require payment by the agency involved of reasonable attorney fees incurred by an employee or applicant for employment if the employee or applicant is the prevailing party and the Board, administrative law judge, or other employee (as the case may be) determines that payment by the agency is warranted in the interest of justice, including any case in which a prohibited personnel practice was engaged in by the agency or any case in which the agency's action was clearly without merit."

5 U.S.C. § 1204(m)(2)

"If an employee or applicant for employment is the prevailing party of a case arising under section 1215 and the decision is based on a finding of discrimination prohibited under section 2302(b)(1) of this title, the payment of attorney fees shall be in accordance with the standards prescribed under section 706(k) of the Civil Rights Act of 1964 (42 U.S.C. 2000e-5(k))."

5 U.S.C. § 1214(g)

"If the Board orders corrective action under this section, such corrective action may include... (2) reimbursement for attorney's fees ..."

5 U.S.C. § 1221(g)(1)(B)

"Corrective action shall include attorney's fees and costs...."

5 U.S.C. § 1221(g)(2)

"If an employee, former employee, or applicant for employment is the prevailing party before the Merit Systems Protection Board, and the decision is based on a finding of a prohibited personnel practice, the agency involved shall be liable to the employee, former employee, or applicant for reasonable attorney's fees and any other reasonable costs incurred."

5 U.S.C. § 1221(g)(3)

"If an employee, former employee, or applicant for employment is the prevailing party in an appeal from the Merit Systems Protection Board, the agency involved shall be liable to the employee, former employee, or applicant for reasonable attorney's fees and any other reasonable costs incurred, regardless of the basis of the decision."

Federal Erroneous Retirement Coverage Corrections Act

5 U.S.C. § 8331 note (Public Law 106-265, § 2208(a)(2))

"The Director of the Office of Personnel Management may... (2) provide for the reimbursement of necessary and reasonable expenses incurred by an individual with respect to settlement of a claim for losses resulting from a retirement coverage error, including attorney's fees, court costs, and other actual expenses...."

Civil Service Reform Act of 1978

5 U.S.C. § 5596(b)(1)

"An employee of an agency who... is found... to have been affected by an unjustified or unwarranted personnel action which has resulted in the withdrawal or reduction of all or a part of the pay, allowances, or differentials of the employee — (A) is entitled, on correction of the personnel action, to receive... (ii) reasonable attorney fees related to the personnel action which... shall be awarded in accordance with standards established under section 7701(g) of this title."

5 U.S.C. § 7701(g)

"(1) Except as provided in paragraph (2) of this subsection, the Board... may require payment by the agency involved of reasonable attorney fees incurred by the employee or applicant for employment if the employee or applicant for employment is the prevailing party and the Board... determines that payment by the agency is warranted in the interest of justice...."

"(2) If an employee or applicant for employment is the prevailing party and the decision is based on a finding of discrimination prohibited under section 2302(b)(l) of this title, the payment of attorney fees shall be in accordance with the standards prescribed under section 706k of the Civil Rights Act of 1964 (42 U.S.C. 2000e-5(k))."

Commodity Exchange Act

7 U.S.C. § 18(c)

"In case a complaint is made by a nonresident of the United States, the complainant shall be required, before any formal action is taken on his complaint, to furnish a bond in double the amount of the claim conditioned upon the payment of costs, including a reasonable attorney's fee for the respondent if the respondent shall prevail...."

7 U.S.C. § 18(d)

"If the petitioner finally prevails, he shall be allowed a reasonable attorney's fee, to be taxed and collected as a part of the costs of the suit."

7 U.S.C. § 18(e)

"If the appellee prevails, he shall be allowed a reasonable attorney's fee to be taxed and collected as a part of his costs."

Packers and Stockyards Act

7 U.S.C. § 210(f)

"If the petitioner finally prevails, he shall be allowed a reasonable attorney's fee to be taxed and collected as a part of the costs of the suit."

Perishable Agricultural Commodities Act

7 U.S.C. § 499f(e)

"In case a complaint is made by a nonresident of the United States ... the complainant shall be required... to furnish a bond... conditioned upon the payment of costs, including a reasonable attorney's fee for respondent if the respondent shall prevail...."

U.S.C. § 499g(b)

"If the petitioner finally prevails, he shall be allowed a reasonable attorney's fee, to be taxed and collected as a part of the costs of the suit."

7 U.S.C. § 499g(c)

"Either party adversely affected by the entry of a reparation order by the Secretary may... appeal therefrom.... Such appeal shall not be effective unless... the appellant also files with the clerk a bond... conditioned upon the payment of the judgment entered by the court, plus interest and costs, including a reasonable attorney's fee for the appellee, if the appellee shall prevail....[I]f appellee prevails he shall be allowed a reasonable attorney's fee to be taxed and collected as a part of his costs."

Federal Crop Insurance Act

7 U.S.C. § 1507(c)

"The Board shall provide such agents and brokers with indemnification, including costs and reasonable attorney fees, from the Corporation for errors or omissions on the part of the Corporation or its contractors for which the agent or broker is sued or held liable, except to the extent the agent or broker has caused the error or omission."

7 U.S.C. § 150 8(j)(3)

"The Corporation shall provide approved insurance providers with indemnification, including costs and reasonable attorney fees incurred by the approved insurance provider, due to errors or omissions on the part of the Corporation."

Animal Welfare Act

7 U.S.C. § 2157(d)

"It shall be unlawful for any member of an Institutional Animal Committee to release any confidential information of the research facility.... Any person, including any research facility, injured in its business or property by reason of a violation of this section may recover all actual and consequential damages sustained by such person and the cost of the suit including a reasonable attorney's fee."

Agricultural Unfair Trade Practices

7 U.S.C. § 2305(a)

"In any action commenced pursuant hereto, the court, in its discretion, may allow the prevailing party a reasonable attorney's fee as part of the costs."

7 U.S.C. § 2305(c)

"In any action commenced pursuant to this subsection, the court may allow the prevailing party a reasonable attorney's fee as a part of the costs."

Plant Variety Act

7 U.S.C. § 2565

"The court in exceptional cases may award reasonable attorney fees to the prevailing party.

7 U.S.C. § 2570(b)

"Such remedies include... attorney fees under section 2565 of this title."

Immigration and Nationality Act

8 U.S.C. § 1324b(h)

"In any complaint respecting an unfair immigration-related employment practice, an administrative law judge, in the judge's discretion, may allow a prevailing party, other than the United States, a reasonable attorney's fee, if the losing party's argument is without reasonable foundation in law and fact."

8 U.S.C. § 1324b(j)(4)

"In any judicial proceeding under subsection (i) of this section or this subsection, the court, in its discretion, may allow a prevailing party, other than the United States, a reasonable attorney's fee as part of the costs but only if the losing party's argument is without reasonable foundation in law and fact."

Gonzales Act

10 U.S.C. § 1089(f)(2)

"With respect to the Secretary of Defense and the Armed Forces Retirement Home Board, the authority provided by paragraph (1) also includes the authority to provide for reasonable attorney's fees for persons described in subsection (a), as determined necessary pursuant to regulations prescribed by the head of the agency concerned." (The persons in question are medical personnel who are sued for malpractice where a suit against the federal government under the Federal Tort Claims Act is the exclusive remedy.)

Whistleblower Protections for Contractor Employees of Department of Defense, Coast Guard, and National Aeronautics and Space Administration

10 U.S.C. § 2409(c)(1)

"If the head of an agency determines that a contractor has subjected a person to a reprisal prohibited by subsection (a), the head of the agency may... (C) Order the contractor to pay the complainant an amount equal to the aggregate of all costs and expenses (including attorneys' fees and expert witnesses' fees) that were reasonably incurred...."

Bankruptcy Act

11 U.S.C. § 110(i)(1)(C)

"[I]f a bankruptcy petition preparer ["a person, other than an attorney or an employee of an attorney"] violates this section or commits any fraudulent, unfair, or deceptive act, the bankruptcy court shall certify that fact to the district court, and the district court... shall order the bankruptcy petition preparer to pay to the debtor... reasonable attorneys' fees and costs in moving for damages under this subsection."

11 U.S.C. § 110(i)(2)

"If the trustee or creditor moves for damages on behalf of the debtor under this subsection, the bankruptcy petition preparer shall be ordered to pay the movant the additional amount of $1,000 plus reasonable attorneys' fees and costs incurred."

11 U.S.C. § 110(j)(3)

"The court shall award to a debtor, trustee, or creditor that brings a successful action under this subsection reasonable attorney's fees and costs of the action, to be paid by the bankruptcy petition preparer."

11 U.S.C. § 303(i)

"[T]he court may grant judgment — (1) against the petitioners and in favor of the debtor for — (B) a reasonable attorney's fee...."

11 U.S.C. § 330(a)(1)

"[T]he court may award to a trustee, an examiner, a professional person employed under section 327 or 1103 — (A) reasonable compensation for actual, necessary services rendered by the trustee, examiner, professional person, or attorney and by any paraprofessional person employed by such person."

11 U.S.C. § 362(h)

"An individual injured by any willful violation of a stay provided by this section shall recover actual damages, including costs and attorneys' fees, and, in appropriate circumstances, punitive damages."

11 U.S.C. § 363(n)

"The trustee may... recover any costs, attorneys' fees or expenses incurred in avoiding such sale or recovering such amount."

11 U.S.C. § 503(b)

"After notice and a hearing, there shall be allowed administrative expenses including — (4) reasonable compensation for professional services rendered by an attorney...."

11 U.S.C. § 506(b)

"To the extent that an allowed secured claim is secured by property the value of which, after any recovery under subsection (c) of this section, is greater than the amount of such claim, there shall be allowed to the holder of such claim, interest upon such claim, and any reasonable fees, costs, or charges provided for under the agreement under which such claim arose." Some courts have interpreted this provision to allow attorneys' fees.

11 U.S.C. § 523(d)

"[T]he court shall grant judgment in favor of the debtor for the costs of, and a reasonable attorney's fee for, the proceeding if the court finds that the position of the creditor was not substantially justified, except that the court shall not award such costs and fees if special circumstances would make the award unjust."

Federal Home Loan Bank Act

12 U.S.C. § 1441a(c)(1l)(B)

"The parties specified in the preceding sentence shall be entitled to reasonable attorney fees upon prevailing in any such judicial action."

Home Owners' Loan Act

12 U.S.C. § 1464(d)(1)(B)(vii)

"Any court having jurisdiction of any proceeding instituted under this section by a savings association, or a director or officer thereof, may allow to any such party reasonable expenses and attorneys' fees. Such expenses and fees shall be paid by the savings association."

12 U.S.C. § 1464(q)(3)

"Any person injured by a violation of paragraph (1) may bring an action... and shall be entitled to recover three times the amount of the damages sustained, and the cost of the suit, including a reasonable attorney's fee."

Housing Act of 1959

12 U.S.C. § 1701q-1(f)

"The monetary judgment may, in the court's discretion, include the attorneys fees and other expenses incurred by the United States in connection with the action."

National Housing Act

12 U.S.C. § 1715k(h)(6)

"In cases of defaults on loans insured under this subsection… the Secretary... may acquire the loan and any security therefor upon reimbursement for such collection costs, court, costs, and attorney fees as may be approved by the Secretary."

12 U.S.C. § 1723i(e) (action to collect civil money penalty)

"The monetary judgment may, in the discretion of the court, include any attorneys fees and other expenses incurred by the United States in connection with the action."

12 U.S.C. § 1735f-14(e) (action to collect civil money penalty)

"The monetary judgment may, in the court's discretion, include the attorneys fees and other expenses incurred by the United States in connection with the action."

12 U.S.C. § 1735f-15(f) (action to collect civil money penalty)

"The monetary judgment may, in the court's discretion, include the attorneys fees and other expenses incurred by the United States in connection with the action."

Federal Credit Union Act

12 U.S.C. § 1786(p)

"Any court having jurisdiction of any proceeding instituted under this section by any credit union or a director, officer, or committee member thereof, may allow to any party such reasonable expenses and attorneys' fees as it deems just and proper, and such expenses and fees shall be paid by the credit union or from its assets."

Federal Deposit Insurance Act

12 U.S.C. § 1818(n)

"Any court having jurisdiction of any proceeding instituted under this section by an insured bank or director or officer thereof, may allow to any such party such reasonable expenses and attorneys' fees as it deems just and proper; and such expenses and fees shall be paid by the bank or from its assets."

Bank Holding Company Act

12 U.S.C. § 1844(f)

"Any court having jurisdiction of any proceeding instituted under this subsection may allow to any such party such reasonable expenses and attorneys' fees as it deems just and proper."

Rank Tying Act

12 U.S.C. § 1975

"Any person who is injured in his business or property by reason of anything forbidden in section 1972 of this title... shall be entitled to recover... a reasonable attorney's fee."

Farm Credit Amendments Act of 1985

12 U.S.C. § 2273

"Any court having jurisdiction of any proceeding instituted under this part by a System institution or a director or officer thereof, may allow to any such party such reasonable expenses and attorneys' fees as it deems just and proper; and such expenses and fees shall be paid by the System institution or from its assets."

Real Estate Settlement Procedures Act

12 U.S.C. § 2605(1)

"Whoever fails to comply with any provision of this section shall be liable to the borrower for each such failure in the following amounts: ... (3) Costs.— In addition to the amounts under paragraph (1) or (2), in the case of any successful action under this section, the costs of the action, together with any attorneys fees incurred in connection with such action as the court may determine to be reasonable under the circumstances.

12 U.S.C. § 2607(d)(5)

"In any private action brought pursuant to this subsection, the court may award to the prevailing party the court costs of the action together with reasonable attorneys fees."

International Banking Act of 1978

12 U.S.C. § 3108(b)(5)

"Any court having jurisdiction of any proceeding instituted under this subsection may allow any party to such proceeding such reasonable expenses and attorneys' fees as the court deems just and proper."

Right to Financial Privacy Act of 1978

12 U.S.C. § 34 17(a)

"Any agency or department of the United States or financial institution obtaining or disclosing financial records or information obtained therein in violation of this chapter is liable to the customer to whom such records relate... (4) in the case of any successful action to enforce liability under this section, the costs of the action together with reasonable attorney's fees as determined by the court."

12 U.S.C. § 3418

"In the event of any successful action [for injunctive relief], costs together with reasonable attorney's fees as determined by the court may be recovered."

Expedited Funds Availability Act

12 U.S.C. § 4010(a)

"[A]ny depository institution which fails to comply with any requirement imposed under this title… is liable… (3) in the case of any successful action to enforce the foregoing liability, [for] the costs of the action, together with a reasonable attorney's fee as determined by the court."

Financial Institutions Anti-Fraud Enforcement Act of 1990

12 U.S.C. § 4246 (see also, 18 U.S.C. § 3059A(e)(2))

"When the United States, through private counsel retained under this subchapter, prevails in any civil action, the court, in its discretion, may allow the United States reasonable attorney's fees and other expenses of litigation as part of the costs."

Truth in Savings Act

12 U.S.C. § 4310(a)(3)

"[A]ny depository institution which fails to comply with any requirement imposed under this subtitle… is liable… in an amount equal to the sum of… (3) in the case of any successful action to enforce any liability under paragraph (1) or (2), the costs of the action, together with a reasonable attorney's fee as determined by the court."

Homeowners Protection Act of 1998

12 U.S.C. § 4907

"Any servicer, mortgagee, or mortgage insurer that violates a provision of this Act shall be liable to each mortgagor to whom the violation relates for... (4) reasonable attorney fees, as determined by the court."

Clayton Act

15 U.S.C. § 15(a)

"[A]ny person who shall be injured in his business or property by reason of anything forbidden in the antitrust laws may sue therefor... and shall recover threefold the damages sustained by him, and the cost of suit, including a reasonable attorney's fee."

15 U.S.C. § 15(b)(1)

"[A]ny person who is a foreign state may not recover under subsection (a) of this section an amount in excess of the actual damages sustained by it, and the cost of suit, including a reasonable attorney's fee."

15 U.S.C. § 15c(a)(2)

"The court shall award the State as monetary relief threefold the total damage sustained as described in paragraph (1) of this subsection, and the cost of suit, including a reasonable attorney's fee."

15 U.S.C. § l5c(d)(2)

"[T]he court may, in its discretion, award a reasonable attorney's fee to a prevailing defendant upon a finding that the State attorney general has acted in bad faith, vexatiously, wantonly, or for oppressive reasons."

15 U.S.C. § 26

"In any action under this section in which the plaintiff substantially prevails the court shall award the cost of suit, including a reasonable attorney's fee, to such plaintiff."

15 U.S.C. § 35(a)

"No damages, interest on damages, costs, or attorney's fees may be recovered under section 15, 15a, or 15c of this title from any local government, or official or employee thereof acting in an official capacity."

15 U.S.C. § 36(a)

"No damages. interest on damages costs, or attorney's fees may be recovered under section 15, 15a, or 15c of this title in any claim against a person based on any official action directed by a local government, or official or employee thereof acting in an official capacity."

Unfair Competition Act

15 U.S.C. § 72

"Any person injured in his business or property by reason of any violation of, or combination or conspiracy to violate, this section, may sue therefor... and shall recover… a reasonable attorney's fee."

Securities Act of 1933

15 U.S.C. § 77k(e)

"In any suit under this or any other section of this subchapter the court may, in its discretion, require an undertaking for the payment of the costs of such suit, including reasonable attorney's fees...."

15 U.S.C. § 77z-1(a)(6) (see also, § 77z-1(a)(7)(C), (c)(3))

"Total attorney's fees and expenses awarded by the court to counsel for the plaintiff class shall not exceed a reasonable percentage of the amount of any damages and prejudgment interest actually paid to the class."

Trust Indenture Act

15 U.S.C. § 77ooo(e)

"The indenture to be qualified may contain provisions to the effect that all parties thereto, including the indenture security holders, agree that the court may in its discretion.... assess reasonable costs, including reasonable attorneys' fees, against any party litigant... ."

15 U.S.C. § 77www(a)

"[T]he court may, in its discretion… assess reasonable costs, including reasonable attorneys' fees, against either party litigant...."

Securities Exchange Act of 1934

15 U.S.C. § 78i(e)

"In any such suit the court may, in its discretion, require an undertaking for the payment of the costs of such suit, and assess reasonable costs, including reasonable attorneys' fees, against either party litigant."

15 U.S.C. § 78r(a)

"In any such suit the court may, in its discretion, require an undertaking for the payment of the costs of such suit, and assess reasonable costs, including reasonable attorneys' fees, against either party litigant."

15 U.S.C. § 78ti(b)(8)

"In the case of an unsuccessful action under paragraph (7), the court shall award the costs of the action and attorney's fees to the Commission if the presiding judge or magistrate finds that the customer's claims were made in bad faith."

Securities Investor Protection Act

15 U.S.C. § 78eee(b)(5)(A)

"The court shall grant reasonable compensation for services rendered and reimbursement for proper costs and expenses incurred... by a trustee, and by the attorney for such trustee, in connection with a liquidation proceeding."

Jewelers' Liability Act

15 U.S.C. § 298(b)

"Any competitor, customer, or competitor of a customer... may sue... and shall recover... a reasonable attorney's fee."

15 U.S.C. § 298(c)

"Any duly organized and existing jewelry trade association shall be entitled to injunctive relief... and if successful shall recover the cost of suit, including a reasonable attorney's fee."

15 U.S.C. § 298(d)

"Any defendant against whom a civil action is brought under the provisions of sections 294 to 300 of this title shall be entitled to recover the cost of defending the suit, including a reasonable attorney's fee, in the event such action is terminated without a finding by the court that such defendant is or has been in violation of sections 294 to 300 of this title."

Lanham (Trademark) Act

15 U.S.C. § 1116(d)(11)

"Any person who suffers damage by reason of a wrongful seizure under this subsection has a cause of action against the applicant for the order under which the seizure was made, and shall be entitled... unless the court finds extenuating circumstances, to recover a reasonable attorney's fee."

15 U.S.C. § 1117(a)

"The court in exceptional cases may award reasonable attorney fees to the prevailing party."

15 U.S.C. § 1117(b)

"In assessing damages under subsection (a) of this section, the court shall, unless the court finds extenuating circumstances, enter judgment for three times such profits or damages, whichever is greater, together with a reasonable attorney's fee...."

15 U.S.C. § 1122

"Such remedies include... costs and attorney's fees under section 35 [15 U.S.C. § 1117]."

Truth in Lending Act

15 U.S.C. § 1640(a)

"[A]ny creditor who fails to comply with any requirement imposed under this part including any requirement under section 1635 this title, or part D or E of this subchapter [the Fair Credit Billing Act or the Consumer Leasing Act] with respect to any person is liable [for]... the costs of the action, together with a reasonable attorney's fee as determined by the court."

Fair Credit Billing Act

15 U.S.C. §§ 1666-1666j

See, 15 U.S.C. § 1640(a)

Consumer Leasing Act

15 U.S.C. § 1667b(a) (see also, 15 U.S.C. § 1640(a))

"In all actions, the lessor shall pay the lessee's reasonable attorney's fees."

Credit Repair Organization Act

15 U.S.C. § 1679g(a)

"Any person who fails to comply with any provision of this title with respect to any other person shall be liable in an amount equal to... (3)... In the case of any successful action to enforce any liability under paragraph (1) or (2), the costs of the action, together with a reasonable attorneys' fee."

Fair Credit Reporting Act

15 U.S.C. § 1681n(c)

"Upon a finding by the court that an unsuccessful pleading, motion, or other paper filed in connection with an action under this section was filed in bad faith or for purposes of harassment, the court shall award to the prevailing party attorney's fees reasonable in relation to the work expended in responding to the pleading, motion, or other paper."

15 U.S.C. § 1681o(b)

"On a finding by the court that an unsuccessful pleading, motion, or other paper filed in connection with an action under this section was filed in bad faith or for purposes of harassment, the court shall award to the prevailing party attorney's fees reasonable in relation to the work expended in responding to the pleading, motion, or other paper."

15 U.S.C. § 1681s(c)(1)

"In addition to such other remedies as are provided under State law, if the chief law enforcement officer of a State, or an official or agency designated by the State, has reason to believe that any person has violated or is violating this title, the State… (C) in the case of any successful action under subparagraph (A) or (B), shall be awarded the costs of the action and reasonable attorney fees as determined by the court."

15 U.S.C. § 1681u(i)

"Any agency or department of the United States obtaining or disclosing any consumer reports, records, or information contained therein in violation of this section is liable to the consumer to whom such consumer reports, records, or information relate in an amount equal to the sum of… (4) in the case of any successful action to enforce liability under this subsection, the costs of the action, together with reasonable attorney fees, as determined by the court."

Equal Credit Opportunity Act

15 U.S.C. § 1691e(d)

"In the case of any successful action under subsection (a), (b), or (c), the costs of the action, together with a reasonable attorney's fee as determined by the court, shall be added to any damages awarded by the court under such subsection."

Fair Debt Collection Practices Act

15 U.S.C. § 1692k(a)

"[A]ny debt collector who fails to comply with any provision of this title with respect to any person is liable [for]… a reasonable attorney's fee as determined by the court. On a finding by the court that an action under this section was brought in bad faith and for the purpose of harassment, the court may award to the defendant attorney's fees reasonable in relation to the work expended and costs."

Electronic Fund Transfer Act

15 U.S.C. § 1693m(a)

"[A]ny person who fails to comply with any provision of this title with respect to any consumer … is liable [for]… a reasonable attorney's fee as determined by the court."

15 U.S.C. § 1693m(f)

"On a finding by the court that an unsuccessful action under this section was brought in bad faith or for purposes of harassment, the court shall award the defendant attorney's fees reasonable in relation to the work expended and costs."

Interstate Land Sales Full Disclosure Act

15 U.S.C. § 1709(c)

"The amount recoverable in a suit authorized by this section may include… reasonable amounts for attorneys' fees."

15 U.S.C. § 1717a(d)

"The monetary judgment may, in the discretion of the court, include any attorneys fees and other expenses incurred by the United States in connection with the action."

Consumer Product Safety Act

15 U.S.C. § 2060(c)

"A court may in the interest of justice include in such relief an award of the costs of the suit, including reasonable attorneys' fees (determined in accordance with subsection (f) of this section) and reasonable expert witnesses' fees. Attorneys' fees may be awarded against the United States (or any agency or official of the United States) without regard to section 2412 of title 28 or any other provision of law."

15 U.S.C. § 2060(f)

"For purposes of this section and sections 2072(a) and 2073 of this title, a reasonable attorney's fee is a fee (1) which is based upon (A) the actual time expended by an attorney in providing advice and other legal services in connection with representing a person in an action brought under this section, and (B) such reasonable expenses as may be incurred by the attorney in the provision of such services, and (2) which is computed at the rate prevailing for the provision of similar services with respect to actions brought in the court which is awarding such fee."

15 U.S.C. § 2072(a)

"Any person who shall sustain injury by reason of any knowing (including willful) violation of a consumer product safety rule ... may, if the court determines it to be in the interest of justice, recover the costs of suit, including reasonable attorneys' fees (determined in accordance with section 2060(f) of this title) and reasonable expert witnesses' fees...."

15 U.S.C. § 2073

"In any action under this section the court may in the interest of justice award the costs of suit, including reasonable attorneys' fees (determined in accordance with section 2060(f) of this title) and reasonable expert witnesses' fees."

Hobby Protection Act

15 U.S.C. § 2102

"In any such action, the court may award the costs of the suit, including reasonable attorneys' fees."

Magnuson-Moss Warranty Act

15 U.S.C. § 2310(d)(2)

"If a consumer finally prevails in any action brought under paragraph (1) of this subsection, he may be allowed by the court to recover as part of the judgment a sum equal to the aggregate amount of cost and expenses (including attorneys' fees based on actual time expended)... unless the court in its discretion shall determine that such an award of attorneys' fees would be inappropriate."

Toxic Substances Control Act

15 U.S.C. § 2618(d)

"The decision of the court in an action commenced under subsection (a), or of the Supreme Court of the United States on review of such a decision, may include an award of costs of suit and reasonable fees for attorneys and expert witnesses if the court determines that such an award is appropriate."

15 U.S.C. § 2619(c)(2)

"The court in issuing any final order in any action brought pursuant to subparagraph (a) may award costs of suit and reasonable fees for attorneys and expert witnesses if the court determines that such an award is appropriate. Any court, in issuing its decision in an action brought to review such an order, may award costs of suit and reasonable fees for attorneys if the court determines that such an award is appropriate."

15 U.S.C. § 2620(b)(4)(C)

"The court in issuing any final order in any action brought pursuant to subparagraph (A) may award costs of suit and reasonable fees for attorneys and expert witnesses if the court determines that such an award is appropriate. Any court, in issuing its decision in an action brought to review such an order, may award costs of suit and reasonable fees for attorneys if the court determines that such an award is appropriate."

15 U.S.C. § 2622(b)(2)(B)

"If such an order issued, the Secretary, at the request of the complainant, shall assess against the person against whom the order is issued a sum equal to the aggregate amount of all costs and expenses (including attorney's fees) reasonably incurred, as determined by the Secretary...."

Petroleum Marketing Practices Act

15 U.S.C. § 2805(d)(1)

"If the franchisee prevails in any action under subsection (a), such franchisee shall be entitled... to reasonable attorney and expert witness fees to be paid by the franchisor, unless the court determines that only nominal damages are to be awarded to such franchisee, in which case the court, in its discretion, need not direct that such fees be paid by the franchisor."

15 U.S.C. § 280 5(d)(3)

"If any action under subsection (a), the court may, in its discretion, direct that reasonable attorney and expert witness fees be paid by the franchisee if the court finds that such action is frivolous."

Condominium and Cooperative Abuse Relief Act of 1980

15 U.S.C. § 3608(d)

"Such relief may include, but shall not be limited to rescission, reformation, restitution, the award of damages and reasonable attorney fees and court costs. A defendant may recover reasonable attorneys' fees if the court determines that the cause of action filed by the plaintiff is frivolous, malicious, or lacking in substantial merit."

15 U.S.C. § 3611(d)

"The amount recoverable under this section may include interest paid, reasonable attorneys' fees, independent engineer and appraisers' fees, and court costs. A defendant may recover reasonable attorneys' fees if the court determines that the cause of action filed by the plaintiff is frivolous, malicious, or lacking in substantial merit."

Export Trading Company Act of 1982

15 U.S.C. § 4016(b)(1)

"Any person who has been injured as a result of conduct engaged in under a certificate of review may bring a civil action for injunctive relief actual damages, the loss of interest or actual damages, and the cost of suit (including a reasonable attorney's fee) for failure to comply with the standards of section 303(a)[15 U.S.C. § 4013 (a)]."

15 U.S.C. § 4016(b)(4)

"In any action brought under paragraph (1), if the court finds that the conduct does comply with the standards of section 303(a) [15 U.S.C. § 4013(a)], the court shall award to the person against whom the claim is brought the cost of suit attributable to defending the claim (including a reasonable attorney's fee)."

National Cooperative Research Act of 1984

15 U.S.C. § 4303(a)

"Notwithstanding section 4 of the Clayton Act (15 U.S.C. 15) and in lieu of the relief specified in such section, any person who is entitled to recovery on a claim under such section shall recover... the cost of suit attributable to such claim, including a reasonable attorney's fee pursuant to section 5 of this Act [15 U.S.C. § 4304]...."

15 U.S.C. § 4303(b)

"Notwithstanding section 4C of the Clayton Act (15 U.S.C. 15c), and in lieu of the relief specified in such section, any State that is entitled to monetary relief on a claim under such section shall recover... the cost of suit attributable to such claim, including a reasonable attorney's fee pursuant to section 4C of the Clayton Act...."

15 U.S.C. § 4303(c)

"Notwithstanding any provision of any State law providing damages for conduct similar to that forbidden by the antitrust laws, any person who is entitled to recover on a claim under such provision shall not recover in excess of... the cost of suit attributable to such claim, including a reasonable attorney's fee pursuant to section 5 of this Act [15 U.S.C. § 4304]...."

15 U.S.C. § 4304(a)

"Notwithstanding sections 4 and 16 of the Clayton Act [15 U.S.C. § § 15 and 26], in any claim under the antitrust laws, or any State law similar to the antitrust laws, based on the conducting of a joint venture, the court shall, at the conclusion of the action — (1) award to a substantially prevailing claimant the cost of suit attributable to such claim, including a reasonable attorney's fee, or (2) award to a substantially prevailing party defending against any such claim the cost of suit attributable to such claim, including a reasonable attorney's fee, if the claim, or the claimant's conduct during the litigation of the claim, was frivolous, unreasonable, without foundation, or in bad faith."

15 U.S.C. § 4304(b)

"The award made under subsection (a) may be offset in whole or in part by an award in favor of any other party for any part of the cost of suit, including a reasonable attorney's fee, attributable to conduct during the litigation by any prevailing party that the court finds to be frivolous, unreasonable, without foundation, or in bad faith."

Telemarketing and Consumer Fraud Abuse and Prevention Act

15 U.S.C. § 6104(d)

"The court, in issuing any final order in any action brought under subsection (a), may award costs of suit and reasonable fees for attorneys and expert witnesses to the prevailing party."

Professional Boxing Safety Act of 1996

15 U.S.C. § 6309(d)

"Any boxer who suffers economic injury as a result of a violation of any provision of this Act may bring an action in the appropriate Federal or State court and recover the damages suffered, court costs, and reasonable attorneys fees and expenses."

National Historic Preservation Act

16 U.S.C. § 470w-4

"In any civil action brought in any United States district court by any interested person to enforce the provisions of sections 470 to 470a, 470b, and 470c to 470w-6 of this title, if such person substantially prevails in such action, the court may award attorneys' fees, expert witness fees, and other costs of participating in such action, as the court deems reasonable."

Endangered Species Act

16 U.S.C. § 1540(g)(4)

"The court, in issuing any final order in any suit brought pursuant to paragraph (1) of this subsection, may award costs of litigation (including reasonable attorney and expert witness fees) to any party, whenever the court determines such award is appropriate."

Public Utility Regulatory Policies Act of 1978

16 U.S.C. § 2632(a)

"[S]uch utility shall be liable to compensate such consumer (pursuant to paragraph (2)) for reasonable attorneys' fees, expert witness fees, and other reasonable costs incurred."

Alaska National Interest Lands Conservation Act

16 U.S.C. § 3117(a) (see also, 43 U.S.C. § 163 1(c)(3))

"Local residents and other persons and organizations who are prevailing parties in an action filed pursuant to this section shall be awarded their costs and attorney's fees."

Federal Cave Resources Protection Act of 1988

16 U.S.C. § 4307(c)

"If any person fails to pay an assessment of a civil penalty... the Attorney General shall bring a civil action in an appropriate United States district court to recover the amount of the penalty assessed (plus costs, attorney's fees, and interest...)."

Copyright Act

17 U.S.C. § 505

"In any civil action under this title, the court in its discretion may allow the recovery of full costs by or against any party other than the United States or an officer thereof. Except as otherwise provided by this title, the court may also award a reasonable attorney's fee to the prevailing party as part of the costs."

17 U.S.C. § 511(b)

"Such remedies include ... costs and attorney's fees under section 505...."

17 U.S.C. § 512(k)

"As used in this section the term 'monetary relief' means damages, costs, attorneys' fees, and any other form of monetary payment."

17 U.S.C. § 911(f)

"In any civil action arising under this chapter, the court in its discretion may allow the recovery of full costs, including reasonable attorneys' fees, to the prevailing party."

17 U.S.C. § 911(g)(2)

"Such remedies include... costs and attorney's fees under subsection (f)."

17 U.S.C. § 1009(c)

"In an action under subsection (a), the court. . . (4) in its discretion may award a reasonable attorney's fee to the prevailing party."

17 U.S.C. § 1203(b)(5)

"In an action brought under subsection (a), the court… in its discretion may award reasonable attorney's fees to the prevailing party."

17 U.S.C. § 1322(b)

"A seller or distributor who suffers damage... may recover such relief as may be appropriate, including… reasonable attorney's fees."

17 U.S.C. § 1323(d)

"In an action for infringement under this chapter, the court may award reasonable attorney's fees to the prevailing party."

17 U.S.C. § 1325

"That amount shall be to compensate the defendant and shall be charged against the plaintiff and paid to the defendant, in addition to such costs and attorney's fees of the defendant as may be assessed by the court."

Firearm Owners' Protection Act

18 U.S.C. § 924(d)(2)(A)

"In any action or proceeding for the return of firearms or ammunition seized under the provisions of this chapter, the court shall allow the prevailing party, other than the United States, a reasonable attorney's fee, and the United States shall be liable therefor."

18 U.S.C. § 924(d)(2)(B)

"In any other action or proceeding under the provisions of this chapter, the court, when it finds that such action was without foundation, or was initiated vexatiously, frivolously, or in bad faith, shall allow the prevailing party, other than the United States, a reasonable attorney's fee, and the United States shall be liable therefor."

18 U.S.C. § 924(d)(2)(D)

"The United States shall be liable for attorneys' fees under this paragraph only to the extent provided in advance by appropriation Acts."

Brady Handgun Violence Prevention Act

18 U.S.C. § 925A

"In any action under this section, the court, in its discretion, may allow the prevailing party a reasonable attorney's fee as part of the costs."

Civil Asset Forfeiture Reform Act of 2000

18 U.S.C. § 983(b)(2)(B)(ii)

"The court shall enter a judgment in favor of the Legal Services Corporation for reasonable attorney fees and costs submitted pursuant to clause (i) and treat such judgment as payable under section 2465 of title 28, United States Code, regardless of the outcome of the case."

18 U.S.C. § 983(b)(3)

"The court shall set the compensation for representation under this subsection, which shall be equivalent to that provided for court-appointed representation under section 3006A of this title."

Major Fraud Act of 1988

18 U.S.C. § 1031(h)

"Any individual who… is… discriminated against in the terms or conditions of employment by an employer because of lawful acts done by the employee on behalf of the employee or others in furtherance of a prosecution under this section... may. in a civil action, obtain all relief necessary to make such individual whole. Such relief shall include… compensation for any special damages sustained as a result of the discrimination, including litigation costs and reasonable attorney's fees."

Organized Crime Control Act of 1970

18 U.S.C. § 1964(c)

"Any person injured in his business or property by reason of a violation of section 1962 of this chapter may ... sue and shall recover... a reasonable attorney's fee...."

Child Abuse Victims' Rights Act of 1986

18 U.S.C. § 2255(a)

"Any minor who is a victim of a violation of section 2241(c), 2242, 2243, 2251, 2251A, 2252, 2252A, 2260, 2421, 2422, or 2423 of this title and who suffers personal injury as a result of such violation may sue in any appropriate United States District Court and shall recover the actual damages such minor sustains and the cost of the suit, including a reasonable attorney's fee."

Safe Streets for Women Act of 1994

18 U.S.C. § 2259(b)(3)(E)

"[T]he court shall order restitution for any offense under this chapter.... The order of restitution under this section shall direct that... the defendant pay to the victim... the full amount of the victim's losses as determined by the court.... [including] attorneys' fees, as well as other costs incurred...."

Safe Homes for Women Act of 1994

18 U.S.C. § 2264(b)(3)(E)

"[T]he court shall order restitution for any offense under this chapter....The order of restitution under this section shall direct that... the defendant pay to the victim the full amount of the victim's losses as determined by the court... [including] attorneys' fees plus any costs incurred in obtaining a civil protective order...."

Antiterrorism Act of 1990

18 U.S.C. § 2333(a)

"Any national of the United States injured in his or her person, property, or business by reason of an act of international terrorism, or his or her estate, survivors, or heirs, may sue therefor in any appropriate district court of the United States and shall recover threefold the damages he or she sustains and the cost of the suit, including attorney's fees."

Wire Interception Act

18 U.S.C. § 2520(b)(3)

"In any action under this section, appropriate relief includes... a reasonable attorney's fee and other litigation costs reasonably incurred."

Electronic Communications Privacy Act of 1986

18 U.S.C. § 2707(b)(3)

"In a civil action under this section appropriate relief includes... a reasonable attorney's fee and other litigation costs reasonably incurred."

18 U.S.C. § 2707(c)

"In the case of a successful action to enforce liability under this section, the court may assess the costs of the action, together with reasonable attorney fees determined by the court."

Video Privacy Protection Act of 1988

18 U.S.C. § 2710(c)(2)(C)

"The court may award... reasonable attorneys' fees and other litigation costs reasonably incurred."

Driver's Privacy Protection Act of 1994

18 U.S.C. § 2724(b)(3)

"The court may award... reasonable attorneys' fees and other litigation costs reasonably incurred."

Criminal Defendants

18 U.S.C. § 3006A note

"[T]he [federal] court, in any criminal case (other than a case in which the defendant is represented by assigned counsel paid for by the public)... may award to a prevailing party, other than the United States, a reasonable attorney's fee and other litigation expenses, where the court finds that the position of the United States was vexatious, frivolous, or in bad faith, unless the court finds that special circumstances make an award unjust. Such awards shall be granted pursuant to the procedures and limitations (but not the burden of proof) provided for an award under section 2412 of title 28, United States Code...."

Financial Institutions Anti-Fraud Enforcement Act of 1990

18 U.S.C. § 3059A(e)(2) (see also, 12 U.S.C. § 4246)

"(1) A person who... is... discriminated against in the terms or conditions of employment by an employer because of lawful acts done by the person on behalf of the person or others in furtherance of a prosecution under any of the sections referred to in subsection (a)... may, in a civil action, obtain all relief necessary to make the person whole. (2) Relief under paragraph (1) shall include... compensation for any special damages sustained as a result of the discrimination, including litigation costs and reasonable attorney's fees."

Authentication of Foreign Documents

18 U.S.C. § 3495(a)

"Every foreign counsel selected pursuant to a commission issued on application of the United States... shall be paid by the United States, such compensation... as [the consular officer] may allow."

Witness Security Reform Act of 1984

18 U.S.C. 3524(d)(6)

"The United States shall be required by the court to pay litigation costs, including reasonable attorneys' fees, incurred by a parent who prevails in enforcing a custody or visitation order; but shall retain the right to recover such costs from the protected person."

Juvenile Delinquency

18 U.S.C. § 5034

"In cases where the juvenile and his parents, guardian, or custodian are financially able to obtain adequate representation but have not retained counsel, the magistrate may assign counsel and order the payment of reasonable attorney's fees or may direct the juvenile, his parents, guardian, or custodian to retain private counsel within a specified period of time."

Higher Education Act of 1965

20 U.S.C. § 1078(c)(6)(B)(i)

"'Administrative costs of collection of loans' means... attorney's fees...."

20 U.S.C. § 1095a(8)

"The court shall award attorneys' fees to a prevailing employee... ."

Individuals with Disabilities Education Act

20 U.S.C. § 1415(i)(3)(B)

"In any action or proceeding brought under this section, the court, in its discretion, may award reasonable attorneys' fees as part of the costs to the parents of a child with a disability who is the prevailing party."

Discrimination Based on Sex or Blindness (Title IX of Public Law 92-3 18)

20 U.S.C. §§ 1681 *et seq.*

See, 42 U.S.C. § 1988(b).

Foreign Service Act of 1980

22 U.S.C. § 4137(b)

If the Board finds that the grievance is meritorious, the Board shall have the authority to direct the Department — (5) to pay reasonable attorney fees to the grievant to the same extent and in the same manner as such fees may be required by the Merit Systems Protection Board under section 7701(g) of Title 5."

Cuban Liberty and Democratic Solidarity (LIBERTAD) Act of 1996

22 U.S.C. § 6082(a)(1)(A)(ii)

"[A]ny person that... traffics in property which was confiscated by the Cuban Government on or after January 1, 1959, shall be liable to any United States national who owns the claim of such property for... court costs and reasonable attorneys' fees."

Indian Arts and Crafts Act of 1990

25 U.S.C. § 305e(b)

"In addition to the relief specified in subsection (a), the court may award punitive damages and the costs of suit and a reasonable attorney's fee."

Indian Self-Determination and Education Assistance Act

25 U.S.C. § 450m-1(c)

"The Equal Access to Justice Act [5 U.S.C. § 504, 28 U.S.C. § 2412] shall apply to administrative appeals... by tribal organizations regarding self-determination contracts."

Navajo and Hopi Indian Relocation Amendments Act of 1980

25 U.S.C. § 640d-27(a)

"In any litigation or court action between or among the Hopi Tribe, the Navajo Tribe and the United States or any of its officials, departments, agencies, or instrumentalities, arising out of the interpretation or implementation of this subchapter, as amended, the Secretary shall pay, subject to the availability of appropriations, attorney's fees, costs and expenses as determined by the Secretary to be reasonable."

25 U.S.C. § 640d-27(b)

"Upon the entry of a final judgment in any such litigation or court action, the court shall award reasonable attorney's fees, costs and expenses to the party, other than the United States or its officials, departments, agencies, or instrumentalities, which prevails or substantially prevails, where it finds that any opposing party has unreasonably initiated or contested such litigation. Any party to whom such an award has been made shall reimburse the United States out of such award to the extent that it has received payments pursuant to subsection (a) of this section."

American Indian Agricultural Resource Management Act

25 U.S.C. § 3713(a)(1)(C)

"[T]he Secretary [of the Interior] shall issue regulations that... establish civil penalties for the commission of trespass on Indian agricultural lands, which provide for... court costs, and attorney fees."

Internal Revenue Code

26 U.S.C. § 6110(f)(4)(A)

"Any person who has exhausted the administrative remedies prescribed pursuant to paragraph (2) with respect to a request for disclosure may file a petition in the United States Tax Court or a complaint in the United States District Court for the District of Columbia.... [T]he provisions of subparagraphs (C), (D), (E), (F), and (G) of section 552 (a)(4) of title 5, United States Code shall apply to any proceeding under this paragraph." (Subparagraph (E) is the attorneys' fees provision of the Freedom of Information Act.)

26 U.S.C. § 6110(i)(2)

"In any suit brought under the provisions of paragraph (l)(A) ...or in any suit brought under subparagraph (1)(B)... the United States shall be liable [for] the costs of the action together with reasonable attorney's fees as determined by the Court."

26 U.S.C. § 6673(a)(1)

"Whenever it appears to the Tax Court that — (A) proceedings before it have been instituted or maintained by the taxpayer primarily for delay, (B) that the taxpayer's position in such proceedings is frivolous or groundless, or (C) that the taxpayer unreasonably failed to pursue available administrative remedies, the Tax Court, in its decision, may require the taxpayer to pay to the United States a penalty not in excess of $25,000."

26 U.S.C. § 6673(a)(2)

"Whenever it appears to the Tax Court that any attorney or other person admitted to practice before the Tax Court has multiplied the proceedings in any case unreasonably and vexatiously, the Tax Court may require — (A) that such attorney or other person pay personally the excess costs, expenses, and attorney's fees reasonably incurred because of such conduct, or (B) if such attorney is appearing on behalf of the Commissioner of Internal Revenue, that the United States pay such excess costs, expenses, and attorneys' fees in the same manner as such an award by a district court."

26 U.S.C. § 6673(b)(1)

"Whenever it appears to the court that the taxpayer's position in the proceedings before the court instituted or maintained by such taxpayer under section 7433 is frivolous or groundless the court may require the taxpayer to pay to the United States a penalty not in excess of $10,000."

26 U.S.C. § 7430(a)

"In any administrative or court proceeding which is brought by or against the United States in connection with the determination, collection, or refund of any tax, interest, or penalty under this title, the prevailing party [other than the United States or any creditor of the taxpayer involved] may [unless the United States establishes that the position of the United States in the proceeding was substantially justified] be awarded a judgment or a settlement for — (1) reasonable administrative costs incurred in connection with such administrative proceeding within the Internal Revenue Service, and (2) for reasonable litigation costs incurred in connection with such court proceeding."

26 U.S.C. § 7431(c)(3)

"[In the ease of a plaintiff which is described in section 7430 (c)(4)(A)(ii),reasonable attorney's fees except that if the defendant is the United States, reasonable attorneys fees may be awarded only if the plaintiff is the prevailing party...."

26 U.S.C. 7434(b)

In any action brought under subsection (a) upon finding of liability on the part of the defendant, the defendant shall be liable to the plaintiff in an amount equal to greater of $5.000 or the sum of — (1) any actual damages... (2) the costs of the action, and (3) in the court's discretion, reasonable attorneys fees."

26 U.S.C. § 9501(d) (see also, 30 U.S.C. § 932(a))

"Amounts in the Black Lung Disability Trust Fund shall be available, as provided by appropriations Acts, for... (7) the reimbursement of operators and insurers for amounts paid by such operators and insurers (other than amounts paid as penalties, interest, or attorney fees) at any time in satisfaction (in whole or in part of any claim denied... before March 1, 1978...."

Judicial Discipline and Removal Reform Act of 1990

28 U.S.C. § 372(c)(16)

"Upon the request of a judge or magistrate whose conduct is the subject of a complaint under this subsection, the judicial council may, if the complaint has been finally dismissed under paragraph 6(C), recommend that the Director of the Administrative Office of the United States Courts award reimbursement, from funds appropriated to the Federal judiciary, for those reasonable expenses, including attorneys' fees, incurred by that judge or magistrate during the investigation which would not have been incurred but for the requirements of this subsection."

Independent Counsel Reauthorization Act of 1987

28 U.S.C. § 593(t)(1) (see also, 5 U.S.C. § 288i(d))

"Upon the request of an individual who is the subject of an investigation conducted by an independent counsel pursuant to this chapter, the division of the court may, if no indictment is brought against such individual pursuant to that investigation, award reimbursement for those reasonable attorney's fees incurred by that individual...."

Judicial Improvements and Access to Justice Act

28 U.S.C. § 655(e)

"In any trial de novo demanded under subsection (a) in which arbitration was done by consent of the parties, a district court may assess costs, as provided in section 1920 of this title, and reasonable attorney fees against the party demanding the trial de novo if — (1) such party fails to obtain a judgment, exclusive of interest and costs, in the court which is substantially more favorable to such party than the arbitration award, and (2) the court determines that the party's conduct in seeking a trail de novo was in bad faith."

Tucker Act

28 U.S.C. §§ 1346(a), 1491

See, 42 U.S.C. § 4654

U.S. Court of Federal Claims — Patent and copyright cases

28 U.S.C. § 1498(a)

"Reasonable and entire compensation shall include the owner's reasonable costs, including reasonable fees for expert witnesses and attorneys, in pursuing the action if the owner is an independent inventor, a nonprofit organization, or an entity that had no more than 500 employees at any time during the 5-year period preceding the use or manufacture of the patented invention by or for the United States. Notwithstanding the preceding sentences, unless the action has been pending for more than 10 years from the time of filing to the time that the owner applies for such costs and fees, reasonable and entire compensation shall not include such costs and fees if the court finds that the position of the United States was substantially justified or that special circumstances make an award unjust."

Parental Kidnapping Prevention Act of 1980

28 U.S.C. § 1738A note

"In furtherance of the purposes of section 1738A of title 28.... State courts are encouraged to... award to the person entitled to custody or visitation... attorneys' fees...."

Jury System Improvements Act of 1978

28 U.S.C. § 1875(d)(2)

"In any action or proceeding under this section, the court may award a prevailing employee who brings such action by retained counsel a reasonable attorney's fee as part of the costs. The court may tax a defendant employer, as costs payable to the court, the attorney fees and expenses incurred on behalf of a prevailing employee, where such costs were expended pursuant to paragraph (1) of this subsection. The court may award a prevailing employer a reasonable attorney's fee as part of the costs only if the court determines that the action is frivolous, vexatious, or brought in bad faith."

Fees and Costs

28 U.S.C. § 1912

"Where a judgment is affirmed by the Supreme Court or a court of appeals, the court in its discretion may adjudge to the prevailing party just damages for his delay, and single or double costs." This provision has been interpreted to permit awards of attorneys' fees. *See,* 50 ALR Fed 652, 67 ALR Fed 319.

28 U.S.C. § 1927

"Any attorney or other person admitted to conduct cases in any court of the United States or any Territory thereof who so multiplies the proceedings in any case unreasonably and vexatiously may be required by the court to satisfy personally the excess costs, expenses, and attorneys' fees reasonably incurred because of such conduct."

Equal Access to Justice Act

28 U.S.C. § 2412 (see also, 5 U.S.C. § 504)

"(a)(l) Except as otherwise specifically provided by statute, a judgment for costs, as enumerated in section 1920 of this title, but not including the fees and expenses of attorneys, may be awarded to the prevailing party in any action brought by or against the United States..."

"(b) Unless expressly prohibited by statute, a court may award reasonable fees and expenses of attorneys, in addition to the costs which may be awarded pursuant to subsection (a), to the prevailing party in any civil action brought by or against the United States... . The United States shall be liable for such fees and expenses to the same extent that any other party would be liable under the common law or under the terms of any statute which specifically provides for such an award."

"(d)(l)(A) Except as otherwise specifically provided by statute, a court shall award to a prevailing party other than the United States fees and other expenses, in addition to any costs awarded pursuant to subsection (a), incurred by that party in any civil action (other than cases sounding in tort), including proceedings for judicial review of agency action, brought by or against the United States... unless the court finds that the position of the United States was substantially justified or that special circumstances make an award unjust."

"(d)(3) In awarding fees and other expenses under this subsection to a prevailing party in any action for judicial review of an adversary adjudication, as defined in subsection (b)(l)(C) of section 504 of title 5, United States Code, or an adversary adjudication subject to the Contract Disputes Act of 1978, the court shall include in that award fees and other expenses to the same extent authorized under subsection (a) of such section, unless the court finds that during such adversary adjudication the position of the United States was substantially justified, or that special circumstances make an award unjust."

"(e) The provisions of this section shall not apply to any costs, fees, and other expenses in connection with any proceedings to which section 7430 of the Internal Revenue Code of 1986 applies...."

Civil Asset Forfeiture Reform Act of 2000

28 U.S.C. § 2465(b)(1)

"Except as provided in paragraph (2), in any civil proceeding to forfeit property under any provision of Federal law in which the claimant substantially prevails, the United States shall be liable for — (A) reasonable attorney fees and other litigation costs reasonably incurred by the claimant."

28 U.S.C. § 2465(b)(2)(C)

"If there are multiple claims to the same property, the United States shall not be liable for costs and attorneys fees associated with any such claim if the United States... (iii) does not cause the claimant to incur additional, reasonable costs or fees...."

28 U.S.C. § 2465(b)(2)(D)

"If the court enters judgment in part for the claimant and in part for the Government, the court shall reduce the award of costs and attorney fees accordingly."

Federal Debt Collection Procedures Act of 1990

28 U.S.C. § 3205(c)(6)

"The court may award a reasonable attorney's fee to the United States and against the garnishee if the writ is not answered within the time specified therein...."

Presidential and Executive Office Accountability Act (see also, 3 U.S .C. § 435)

28 U.S.C. § 3905(a)

"If a covered employee, with respect to any claim under chapter 5 of title 3, or a qualified person with a disability, with respect to any claim under section 421 of title 3, is a prevailing party in any proceeding under section 1296 or section 1346(g), the court may award attorney's fees, expert fees, and other costs as would be appropriate if awarded under section 706(k) of the Civil Rights Act of 1964."

Assumption of Contractual Obligations Related to Transfers of Rights in Motion Pictures

28 U.S.C. § 4001(g)

"[T]he court in its discretion may allow recovery of full costs by or against any party and may also award a reasonable attorney's fees to the prevailing party as part of the costs."

Federal Rules of Civil Procedure 28 U.S.C. App. Rule 11(c)(2)

"[T]he sanction may consist of, or include… an order directing payment to the movant of some or all of the reasonable attorneys' fees and other expenses incurred as a direct result of the violation."

28 U.S.C. App. Rule 16(f)

"[T]he judge shall require the party or the attorney representing the party or both to pay the reasonable expenses incurred because of any noncompliance with this rule, including attorney's fees, unless the judge finds that the noncompliance was substantially justified or that other circumstances make an award of expenses unjust."

28 U.S.C. App. Rule 26(g)(3)

"If without substantial justification a certification is made in violation of the rule, the court, upon motion or upon its own initiative, shall impose upon the person who made the certification, the party on whose behalf the disclosure, request, response, or objection is made, or both, an appropriate sanction, which may include an order to pay the amount of the reasonable expenses incurred because of the violation, including a reasonable attorney's fee."

28 U.S.C. App. Rule 30(g)(1)

"If the party giving notice of a deposition fails to attend and proceed therewith and another party attends in person or by attorney pursuant to the notice, the court may order the party giving notice to pay to such other party the reasonable expenses incurred by that party and that party's attorney in attending, including reasonable attorney's fees."

28 U.S.C. App. Rule 30(g)(2)

"If the party giving the notice of the taking of the deposition of a witness fails to serve a subpoena on him and the witness because of such failure does not attend, and if another party attends in person or by attorney because that party expects the deposition of that witness to be taken, the court may order the party giving the notice to pay to such other party the reasonable expenses incurred by that party and the party's attorney in attending, including reasonable attorney's fees."

28 U.S.C. App. Rule 37(a)(4)

"(A) If the motion is granted or if the disclosure or requested discovery is provided after the motion was filed, the court shall, after affording an opportunity to be heard require the party or deponent whose conduct necessitated the motion or the party or attorney advising such conduct or both of them to pay to the moving party the reasonable expenses incurred in making the motion, including attorney's fees, unless the court finds...."

"(B) If the motion is denied, the court may enter any protective order authorized under Rule 26(c) and shall, after affording an opportunity to be heard, require the moving party or the attorney filing the motion or both of them to pay to the party or deponent who opposed the motion the reasonable expenses incurred in opposing the motion, including attorney's fees, unless the court finds...."

28 U.S.C. App. Rule 37(b)(2)

"In lieu of any of the foregoing orders or in addition thereto, the court shall require the party failing to obey the order or the attorney advising that party or both to pay the reasonable expenses, including attorney's fees, caused by the failure, unless the court finds...."

28 U.S.C. App. Rule 37(c)(1)

"In addition to requiring payment of reasonable expenses, including attorney's fees, caused by the failure, these sanctions may include...."

28 U.S.C. App. Rule 37(c)(2)

"If a party fails to admit the genuineness of any document or the truth of any matter as requested under Rule 36, and if the party requesting the admissions thereafter proves the genuineness of the document or the truth of the matter, the requesting party may apply to the court for an order requiring the other party to pay the reasonable expenses incurred in making the proof, including reasonable attorney's fees...."

28 U.S.C. App. Rule 37(d)

"In lieu of any order or in addition thereto, the court shall require the party failing to act or the attorney advising that party or both to pay the reasonable expenses, including attorney's fees, caused by the failure, unless the court finds that the failure was substantially justified or that other circumstances make an award of expenses unjust."

28 U.S.C. App. Rule 37(g)

"If a party or a party's attorney fails to participate in good faith in the development and submission of a discovery plan by agreement as required by Rule

26(f), the court may, after opportunity for hearing, require such party or attorney to pay to any other party the reasonable expenses, including attorney's fees, caused by the failure."

28 U.S.C. App. Rule 56(g)

"[T]he court shall forthwith order the party... to pay to the other party the amount of the reasonable expenses which the filing of the affidavits caused him to incur, including reasonable attorney's fees...."

28 U.S.C. App. Rule 68

If, more than ten days before trial begins, a party defending a claim makes a settlement offer which is rejected by the offeree, and, "[i]f the judgment finally obtained by the offeree is not more favorable than the offer, the offeree must pay the costs incurred after the making of the offer." In *Marek v. Chesny,* 473 U.S. 1(1985), the Supreme Court held that "costs" includes attorneys' fees in actions brought under statutes that allow attorneys' fees as part of the costs.

Federal Rules of Appellate Procedure

28 U.S.C. App. Rule 38

"If a court of appeals determines that an appeal is frivolous, it may, after a separately filed motion or notice from the court and reasonable opportunity to respond, award just damages and single or double costs to the appellee." This provision has been interpreted to permit awards of attorneys' fees. *See,* 50 ALR Fed 652, 67 ALR Fed 319.

Norris-La Guardia Act

29 U.S.C. § 107(e)

"No temporary restraining order or temporary injunction shall be issued except on condition that complainant shall first file an undertaking with adequate security in an amount to be fixed by the court sufficient to recompense those enjoined for any loss, expense, or damage caused by the improvident or erroneous issuance of such order or injunction, including all reasonable costs (together with a reasonable attorney's fee)...."

Fair Labor Standards Act

29 U.S.C. § 216(b)

"The court in such action shall, in addition to any judgment awarded to the plaintiff or plaintiffs, allow a reasonable attorney's fee to be paid by the defendant, and costs of the action."

Labor-Management Reporting and Disclosure Act of 1959

29 U.S.C. § 431(c)

"The court in such action may, in its discretion, in addition to any judgment awarded to the plaintiff or plaintiffs, allow a reasonable attorney's fee to be paid by the defendant, and costs of the action."

29 U.S.C. § 501(b)

"The trial judge may allot a reasonable part of the recovery in any action under this subsection to pay the fees of counsel prosecuting the suit...."

Age Discrimination in Employment Act of 1967

29 U.S.C. § 626(b)

This section incorporates the attorneys' fees provision of the Fair Labor Standards Act, 29 U.S.C. 216(b).

Rehabilitation Act of 1973

29 U.S.C. § 794a(b)

"In any action or proceeding to enforce or charge a violation of a provision of this title, the court, in its discretion, may allow the prevailing party, other than the United States, a reasonable attorney's fee as part of the costs."

Employee Retirement Income Security Act

29 U.S.C. § 1132(g)

"In any action under this subchapter by a participant, beneficiary, or fiduciary, the court in its discretion may allow a reasonable attorney's fee and costs of the action to either party."

29 U.S.C. § 1305(b)(1)

"Each fund established under this section shall be credited with the appropriate portion of... (F) attorney's fees awarded to the corporation..."

29 U.S.C. § 1370(e)

"(1) General Rule. — In any action brought under this section, the court in its discretion may award all or a portion of the costs and expenses incurred in connection with such action, including reasonable attorney's fees, to any party who prevails or substantially prevails in such action."

"(2) Exemption for Plans. — Notwithstanding the preceding provisions of this subsection, no plan shall be required in any action to pay any costs and expenses (including attorney's fees)."

29 U.S.C. § 1401(a)(2)

"The arbitrator may also award reasonable attorney's fees."

29 U.S.C. § 1451(e)

"In any action under this section, the court may award all or a portion of the costs and expenses incurred in connection with such action, including reasonable attorney's fees, to the prevailing party."

Employee Polygraph Protection Act of 1988

29 U.S.C. § 2005(c)(3)

"The court, in its discretion, may allow the prevailing party (other than the United States) reasonable costs, including attorney's fees."

Worker Adjustment and Retraining Notification Act

29 U.S.C. § 2104(a)(6)

"In any such suit, the court, in its discretion, may allow the prevailing party a reasonable attorney's fee as part of the costs."

Family and Medical Leave Act of 1993

29 U.S.C. § 2617(a)(3)

"The court in such an action shall, in addition to any judgment awarded to the plaintiff, allow a reasonable attorney's fee, reasonable expert witness fees, and other costs of the action to be paid by the defendant."

Federal Coal Mine Health and Safety Act of 1969

30 U.S.C. § 815(c)(3)

"Whenever any order is issued sustaining the complainant's charges under this subsection, a sum equal to the aggregate amount of all costs and expenses (including attorney's fees)... shall be assessed against the person committing such violation."

30 U.S.C. § 932(a) — Black Lung Benefits Act *(see also,* 26 U.S.C. § 9501(d)(7))

This subsection incorporates 33 U.S.C. § 928(a) and (b).

30 U.S.C. § 938(c)

"Whenever an order is issued under this subsection granting relief to a miner at the request of such miner, a sum equal to the aggregate amount of all costs and expenses (including attorney's fees)… shall be assessed against the person committing the violation."

Surface Mining control and Reclamation Act

30 U.S.C. § 1270(d)

"The court, in issuing any final order in any action brought pursuant to subsection (a) of this section, may award costs of litigation (including attorney and expert witness fees) to any party, whenever the court determines such award is appropriate."

30 U.S.C. § 1270(f)

"Any person who is injured in his person or property through the violation by any operator of any rule, regulation, order, or permit issued pursuant to this chapter may bring an action for damages (including reasonable attorney and expert witness fees)...."

30 U.S.C. § 1275(e)

"Whenever an order is issued under this section, or as a result of any administrative proceeding under this chapter, at the request of any person, a sum equal to the aggregate amount of all costs and expenses (including attorney fees)... may be assessed against either party...."

30 U.S.C. § 1293(c)

"Whenever an order is issued under this Section to abate any violation, at the request of the applicant a sum equal to the aggregate amount of all costs and expenses (including attorneys' fees)... shall be assessed against the persons committing the violation."

Deep Seabed Hard Mineral Resources Act

30 U.S.C. § 1427(c)

"The court, in issuing any final order in any action brought under subsection (a) of this section, may award costs of litigation, including reasonable attorney and expert witness fees, to any party whenever the court determines that such an award is appropriate."

General Accounting Office Act of 1980

31 U.S.C. § 755(b)

"If an officer, employee, applicant for employment, or employee of the Architect of the Capitol, the Botanic Garden, or the Senate Restaurants is the prevailing party in a proceeding under this section, and the decision is based on a finding of discrimination prohibited under section 732(f) of this title or section 312(e)(2) of the Architect of the Capitol Human Resources Act, attorneys fees may be allowed by the court in accordance with the standards prescribed under section 706(k) of the Civil Rights Act of 1964 [42 U.S.C. § 2000e-5(k)]."

Federal Acquisition Streamlining Act of 1994

31 U.S.C. § 3554(c)(1)

"If the Comptroller General determines that a solicitation for a contract or a proposed award or the award of a contract does not comply with a statute or regulation, the Comptroller General may recommend that the Federal agency conducting the procurement pay to an appropriate interested party the costs of — (A) filing and pursuing the protest, including reasonable attorneys' fees and consultant and expert witness fees...."

31 U.S.C. § 3554(c)(2)

"No party... may be paid, pursuant to a recommendation made under the authority of paragraph (1) — (A) costs for consultant and expert witness fees that exceed the highest rate of compensation for expert witnesses paid by the Federal Government; or (B) costs for attorneys' fees that exceed $150 per hour unless the agency determines, based on the recommendation of the Comptroller General on a case by case basis, that an increase in the cost of living or a special factor, such as the limited availability of qualified attorneys for the proceedings involved, justifies a higher fee."

Debt Collection Improvement Act of 1996

31 U.S.C. § 3720D(e)(2)

"The court shall award attorneys' fees to a prevailing employee...."

31 U.S.C. § 3720D(f)(1)(B)

"The employer of an individual... shall be liable for any amount that the employer fails to withhold from wages due an employee following receipt by such employer of notice of the withholding order, plus attorneys' fees, costs, and, in the court's discretion, punitive damages."

False Claims Act

31 U.S.C. § 3730(d)(1)

"Any such person shall also receive an amount for reasonable expenses which the court finds to have been necessarily incurred, plus reasonable attorneys' fees and costs. All such expenses, fees, and costs shall be awarded against the defendant."

31 U.S.C. § 3730(d)(2)

"Such person shall also receive an amount for reasonable expenses which the court finds to have been necessarily incurred, plus reasonable attorneys' fees and costs. All such expenses, fees, and costs shall be awarded against the defendant."

31 U.S.C. § 3730(d)(4)

"[T]he court may award to the defendant its reasonable attorneys' fees and expenses if the defendant prevails in the action and the court finds that the claim of the person bringing the action was clearly frivolous, clearly vexatious, or brought primarily for purposes of harassment."

31 U.S.C. § 3730(g)

"In civil actions brought under this section by the United States, the provisions of section 2412(d) of title 28 shall apply."

31 U.S.C. § 3730(h)

"Such relief shall include... litigation costs and reasonable attorneys' fees."

Local Partnership Act

31 U.S.C. § 6716(c)

"In an action under this section, the court... to enforce compliance with section 6711(a) or (b), may allow a prevailing party (except the United States Government) a reasonable attorney's fee."

Longshore and Harbor Workers' Compensation Act

33 U.S.C. § 928(a)

"[T]here shall be awarded, in addition to the award of compensation, in a compensation order, a reasonable attorney's fee against the employer or carrier in an amount approved by the deputy commissioner, the Board, or court, as the case may be...."

33 U.S.C. § 928(b)

"[A] reasonable attorney's fee based solely upon the difference between the amount awarded and the amount tendered or paid shall be awarded in addition to the amount of compensation.... If the claimant is successful in review proceedings before the Board or court in any such case an award may be made in favor of the claimant and against the employer or carrier for a reasonable attorney's fee for claimant's counsel...."

33 U.S.C. § 933(e)(1)

"The employer shall retain an amount equal to — (A) the expenses incurred by him in respect to such proceedings or compromise (including a reasonable attorney's fee) as determined by the deputy commissioner or Board...."

Water Pollution Prevention and Control Act

33 U.S.C. § 1319(g)(9)

"Any person who fails to pay on a timely basis the amount of an assessment of a civil penalty as described in the first sentence of this paragraph shall be required to pay, in addition to such amount and interest, attorneys fees and costs for collection proceedings...."

33 U.S.C. § 1321(b)(6)(H)

"Any person who fails to pay on a timely basis the amount of an assessment of a civil penalty as described in the first sentence of this subparagraph shall be required to pay, in addition to such amount and interest, attorneys fees and costs for collection proceedings...."

33 U.S.C. § 1365(d)

"The court in assuming any final order in any action brought pursuant to this section may award costs of litigation (including reasonable attorney and expert witness fees to any prevailing or substantially prevailing party, whenever the court determines such award is appropriate."

33 U.S.C. § 1367 (c)

"[A] sum equal to the aggregate amount of all costs and expenses (including the attorney's fees), as determined by the Secretary of Labor... shall be assessed against the person committing such violation."

33 U.S.C. § 1369(b)(3)

"In any judicial proceeding under this subsection, the court may award costs of litigation (including reasonable attorney and expert witness fees) to any prevailing or substantially prevailing party whenever it determines that such award is appropriate."

Marine Protection, Research, and Sanctuaries Act

33 U.S.C. § 1415(g)(4)

"The court, in issuing any final order in any suit brought pursuant to paragraph (1) of this subsection may award costs of litigation (including reasonable attorney and expert witness fees) to any party, whenever the court determines such award is appropriate."

Deep Water Ports Act

33 U.S.C. § 1515(d)

"The court, in issuing any final order in any action brought pursuant to subsection (a) of this section, may award costs of litigation (including reasonable attorney and expert witness fees) to any party, whenever the court determines such award is appropriate."

Act to Prevent Pollution from Ships

33 U.S.C. § 1910(d)

"The court, in issuing any final order in any action brought pursuant to this section may award costs of litigation (including reasonable attorney and expert witness fees) to any party including the Federal Government."

Oil Pollution Act of 1990

33 U.S.C. § 2715(c)

"At the request of the Secretary, the Attorney General shall commence an action on behalf of the Fund to recover any compensation paid by the Fund to any claimant pursuant to this chapter, and all costs incurred by the Fund by reason of the claim, including... attorney's fees."

Patent Infringement

35 U.S.C. § 271 (e)(4)

"The remedies prescribed by subparagraphs (A), (B), and (C) are the only remedies which maybe granted by a court for an act of infringement described in paragraph (2), except that a court may award attorney fees under section 285."

35 U.S.C. § 285

"The court in exceptional cases may award reasonable attorney fees to the prevailing party."

35 U.S.C. § 296(b)

"Such remedies include... attorney fees under [35 U.S.C.] section 285...."

Amateur Sports Act of 1978 (use of Olympic symbols)

36 U.S.C. § 380(a)

This provision incorporates the attorneys' fees provision of the Trademark Act, 15 U.S.C.§ 1117. *See, International Olympic Committee v. San Francisco Arts & Athletics,* 781 F.2d 733 (9th Cir. 1986). *rehearing denied,* 781 F.2d 733 (9th Cir.

1986), *rehearing denied*, 789 F.2d 1319 (9th Cir. 1986), *aff'd* (not on an attorneys' fees issue), 483 U.S. 522 (1987).

Uniformed Services Employment and Reemployment Rights Act of 1994

38 U.S.C. § 4323(c)(2)(B)

"In any action or proceeding to enforce a provision of this chapter by a person under subsection (a)(2) who obtained private counsel for such action or proceeding, the court may award any such person who prevails in such action or proceeding reasonable attorney fees, expert witness fees, and other litigation expenses."

Federal Acquisition Streamlining Act of 1994

41 U.S.C. § 265(c)(1)

"If the head of an executive agency determines that a contractor has subjected a person to a reprisal prohibited by subsection (a), the head of the executive agency may … (C) Order the contractor to pay the complainant an amount equal to the aggregate amount of all costs and expenses (including attorneys' fees and expert witnesses' fees) that were reasonably incurred...."

Contract Disputes Act of 1978

41 U.S.C. §§ 601 *et seq.*

See, 28 U.S.C. § 2412(d)(3)

Safe Drinking Water Act

42 U.S.C. § 300h-2(c)(7)

"If any person fails to pay an assessment of a civil penalty… the Administrator may request the Attorney General to bring a civil action in an appropriate district court to recover the amount assessed (plus costs, attorneys' fees, and interest…)."

42 U.S.C. § 300j-8(d)

"The court, in issuing any final order in any action brought under subsection (a) of this section, may award costs of litigation (including reasonable attorney and expert witness fees) to any party whenever the court determines such an award is appropriate."

42 U.S.C. § 300j-9(i)(2)(B)(ii)

"If such an order is issued, the Secretary, at the request of the complainant, shall assess against the person against whom the order is issued a sum equal to the aggregate amount of all costs and expenses (including attorneys' fees) reasonably incurred...."

National Childhood Vaccine Injury Act of 1986

42 U.S.C. § 300aa-15(b)

"Compensation awarded under the [National Vaccine Injury Compensation] Program... may also include an amount not to exceed a combined total of $30,000 for — (1) lost earnings... (2) pain and suffering... , and (3) reasonable attorneys' fees and costs (as provided in subsection (e) of this section."

42 U.S.C. § 300aa-15(e)

"(1) In awarding compensation on a petition filed under section 300aa-11 of this title the special master or court shall also award as part of such compensation an amount to cover — (A) reasonable attorneys' fees, and (B) other costs, incurred in any proceeding on such petition. If the judgment of the United States Court of Federal Claims on such a petition does not award compensation, the special master or court may award an amount of compensation to cover petitioner's reasonable attorneys' fees and other costs incurred in any proceeding on such petition if the special master or court determines that the petition was brought in good faith and there was a reasonable basis for the claim for which the petition was brought."

"(2) If the petitioner, before the effective date of this subpart, filed a civil action for damages for any vaccine-related injury or death for which compensation may be awarded under the Program, and petitioned under section 300aa- 11 (a)(5) of this title to have such action dismissed and to file a petition for compensation under the Program, in awarding compensation on such petition the special master or court may include an amount of compensation limited to the costs and expenses incurred by the petitioner and the attorney of the petitioner before the effective date of this subpart in preparing, filing, and prosecuting such civil action (including the reasonable value of the attorney's time if the civil action was filed under contingent fee arrangements)."

42 U.S.C. § 300aa-31(c)

"The court, in issuing any final order in any action under this section, may award costs of litigation (including reasonable attorney and expert witness fees) to any plaintiff who substantially prevails on one or more significant issues in the action."

Social Security Act

42 U.S.C. § 669a(c)

"In any action brought under paragraph (1), upon a finding of liability on the part of the defendant, the defendant shall be liable to the plaintiff in an amount equal to the sum of... (B) the costs (including attorney's fees) of the action."

42 U.S.C. § 673(a)(6)(A)

"For purposes of paragraph (l)(B)(i), the term non-recurring adoption expenses' means reasonable and necessary adoption fees, court costs, attorney fees, and other expenses which are directly related to the legal adoption of a child with special needs and which are not incurred in violation of State or Federal law."

42 U.S.C. § 1320a-8(b)(4)(G)

"The official conducting a hearing under this section may sanction a person, including any party or attorney.... Such sanction may include... ordering the party or attorney to pay the attorneys' fees and other costs caused by the failure or misconduct...."

United States Housing Act of 1937

42 U.S.C. § 1437d(q)(7)

"Appropriate relief that may be awarded by such district courts shall include reasonable attorney's fees and other litigation costs."

Civil Money Penalties against Section 8 Owners

42 U.S.C. § 1437z-1(e)(1)(B)

"Any monetary judgment awarded in an action brought under this paragraph may, in the discretion of the court, include the attorney's fees and other expenses incurred by the United States in connection with the action."

Homeownership and Opportunity through HOPE Act

42 U.S.C. § 1437aaa-4(h) (*see also*, 42 U.S.C. §§ 12875, 12895)

"The parties specified in the preceding sentence shall be entitled to reasonable attorney fees upon prevailing in any such judicial action."

Housing Act of 1949

42 U.S.C. *§* 1490s (added by P.L. 106-569, § 708)

"The monetary judgment may, in the court's discretion, include the attorney's fees and other expenses incurred by the United States in connection with the action."

Voting Rights Act of 1965

42 U.S.C. § 1973l(e)

"In any action or proceeding to enforce the voting guarantees of the fourteenth or fifteenth amendment, the court, in its discretion, may allow the prevailing party, other than the United States, a reasonable attorney's fee as part of the costs."

Voting Accessibility for the Elderly and Handicapped Act

42 U.S.C. § 1973ee-4(c)

"Notwithstanding any other provision of law, no award of attorney fees may be made with respect to an action under this section, except in any action brought to enforce the original judgment of the court."

National Voter Registration Act of 1993

42 U.S.C. § 1973gg-9(c)

"In a civil action under this section, the court may allow the prevailing party (other than the United States) reasonable attorney fees, including litigation expenses, and costs."

Civil Rights Attorney's Fees Awards Act of 1976

42 U.S.C. § 1988(b)

"In any action or proceeding to enforce a provision of sections 1981, 1981a, 1982, 1983, 1985, and 1986 of this title, title IX of Public Law 92-318, the Religious Freedom Restoration Act of 1993, the Religious Land Use and Institutionalized Persons Act of 2000, title VI of the Civil Rights Act of 1964, or section 40302 of the Violence Against Women Act of 1994, the court, in its discretion, may allow the prevailing party, other than the United States, a reasonable attorney's fee as part of the costs, except that in any action brought against a judicial officer for an act or omission taken in such officer's judicial capacity such officer shall not be held liable for any costs, including attorney's fees, unless such action was clearly in excess of such officer's jurisdiction."

Civil Rights Act of 1991

42 U.S.C. § 1988(c)

"In awarding an attorney's fee under subsection (b) of this section in any action or proceeding to enforce a provision of section 1981 or 1981a of this title, the court, in its discretion, may include expert fees as part of the attorney's fee."

Civil Rights of Institutionalized Persons Act

42 U.S.C. § 1997a(b)

"In any action commenced under this section, the court may allow the prevailing party, other than the United States, a reasonable attorney's fee against the United States as part of the costs."

42 U.S.C. § 1997c(d)

"In any action in which the United States joins as an intervenor under this section, the court may allow the prevailing party, other than the United States, a reasonable attorney's fee against the United States as part of the costs.. ."

42 U.S.C. § 1997e(d)

"In an action brought by a prisoner who is confined to any jail, prison, or other correctional facility, in which attorney's fees are authorized under section 1988 of this title, such fees shall not be awarded, except to the extent that...."

Civil Rights Act of 1964, Title II

42 U.S.C. § 2000a-3(b)

"In any action commenced pursuant to this subchapter, the court, in its discretion, may allow the prevailing party, other than the United States, a reasonable attorney's fee as part of the costs, and the United States shall be liable for costs the same as a private party."

Civil Rights Act of 1964, Title III

42 U.S.C. § 2000b-1

"In any action or proceeding under this subchapter the United States shall be liable for costs, including a reasonable attorney's fee, the same as a private party."

Civil Rights Act of 1964, Title VII

42 U.S.C. § 2000e-5(g)(2)(B)

"On a claim in which an individual proves a violation under section 703(m) [42 U.S.C. § 2000e-2(m)] and a respondent demonstrates that the respondent would have taken the same action in the absence of the impermissible motivating factor, the court — (i) may grant declaratory relief, injunctive relief (except as provided in clause (ii)), and attorney's fees and costs demonstrated to be directly attributable only to the pursuit of the claim under section 703(m)...."

42 U.S.C. § 2000e-5(k)

"In any action or proceeding under this subchapter the court, in its discretion, may allow the prevailing party, other than the [Equal Employment Opportunity] Commission or the United States, a reasonable attorney's fee (including expert fees) as part of the costs, and the Commission and the United States shall be liable for costs the same as a private person."

Privacy Protection Act of 1980

42 U.S.C. § 2000aa-6(f)

"A person having a cause of action under this section shall be entitled to recover such reasonable attorneys' fees and other litigation costs reasonably incurred as the court, in its discretion, may award...."

Atomic Energy Act of 1954

42 U.S.C. § 2184

"If in any action against such patent licensee, the court shall determine that the defendant is exercising such license, the measure of damages shall be the royalty fee determined pursuant to section 2187(c) of this title, together with such costs, interest and reasonable attorney's fees as may be fixed by the court... . If any such patent licensee shall fail to pay such royalty fee, the patentee may bring an action in any court of competent jurisdiction for such royalty fee, together with such costs, interest and reasonable attorney's fees as may be fixed by the court."

Legal Services Corporation Act

42 U.S.C. § 2996e(f)

"If an action is commenced by the Corporation or by a recipient and a final order is entered in favor of the defendant and against the Corporation or a recipient's plaintiff, the court shall, upon motion by the defendant and upon a finding by the court that the action was commenced or pursued for the sole purpose of harassment of the defendant or that the Corporation or a recipient's plaintiff maliciously abused legal process, enter an order (which shall be appealable before being made final) awarding reasonable costs and legal fees incurred by the defendant in defense of the action, except when in contravention of a State law, a rule or court, or a statute of general applicability. Any such costs and fees shall be directly paid by the Corporation."

Department of Housing and Urban Development Act

42 U.S.C. § 3537a(c)(5)

"The monetary judgment may, in the court's discretion, include the attorneys' fees and other expenses incurred by the United States in connection with the action."

42 U.S.C. § 3544(c)(3)

"Appropriate relief that may be ordered by such district courts shall include reasonable attorney's fees and other litigation costs."

42 U.S.C. § 3545(i)

"The monetary judgment may, in the court's discretion, include the attorneys' fees and other expenses incurred by the United States in connection with the action."

Fair Housing Act

42 U.S.C. § 3612(p)

"In any administrative proceeding brought under this section, or any court proceeding arising therefrom, or any civil action under section 812 [42 U.S.C.§ 3612], the administrative law judge or the court as the case may be, in its discretion, may allow the prevailing party, other than the United States, a reasonable attorney's fee and costs. The United States shall be liable for such fees and costs to the extent provided by section 504 of title 5, United States Code, or by section 2412 of title 28, United States Code."

42 U.S.C. § 3613(c)(2)

"In a civil action under subsection (a), the court, in its discretion, may allow the prevailing party, other than the United States, a reasonable attorney's fee and costs. The United States shall be liable for such fees and costs to the same extent as a private person."

42 U.S.C. § 3614(d)(2)

"In a civil action [by the Attorney General] under this section, the court, in its discretion, may allow the prevailing party, other than the United States, a reasonable attorney's fee and costs. The United States shall be liable for such fees and costs to the extent provided by section 2412 of title 28, United States Code."

Omnibus Crime Control and Safe Streets Act of 1968

42 U.S.C. § 3789d(c)(4)(B)

"In any civil action brought by a private person to enforce compliance with any provision of this subsection, the court may grant to a prevailing plaintiff reasonable attorney fees, unless the court determines that the lawsuit is frivolous, vexatious, brought for harassment purposes, or brought principally for the purpose of gaining attorney fees."

National Flood Insurance Act of 1968

42 U.S.C. § 4081(c)

"The Director of the Federal Emergency Management Agency... shall provide any such agent or broker with indemnification, including court costs and reasonable attorney fees, arising out of and caused by an error or omission on the part of the Federal Emergency Management Agency and its contractors."

Uniform Relocation Assistance and Real Property Acquisition Policies Act

42 U.S.C. § 4654

"(a) The Federal court… shall award… such a sum as will in the opinion of the court reimburse such owner for his reasonable costs, disbursements, and expenses, including reasonable attorney, appraisal, and engineering fees, actually incurred because of the condemnation proceedings, if...."

"(c) The court rendering a judgment for the plaintiff in a proceeding brought under Section 1346(a)(2) or 1491 of Title 28, awarding compensation for the taking of property by a Federal agency., or the Attorney General effecting a settlement of any such proceeding, shall determine and award or allow to such plaintiff… reasonable attorney, appraisal, and engineering fees, actually incurred because of such proceeding."

Noise Control Act of 1972

42 U.S.C. § 4911(d)

"The court, in issuing any final order in any action brought pursuant to subsection (a) of this section, may award costs of litigation (including reasonable attorney and expert witness fees) to any party, whenever the court determines such an award is appropriate."

National Manufactured Housing Construction and Safety Standards Act

42 U.S.C. § 5412(b)

"[T]he person bringing the action shall also be entitled to recover any damage sustained by him, as well as all court costs plus reasonable attorneys' fees."

Energy Reorganization Act of 1974

42 U.S.C. § 5851(b)(2)(B)

"If an order is issued under this paragraph, the Secretary, at the request of the complainant shall assess against the person against whom the order is issued a sum equal to the aggregate amount of all costs and expenses (including attorneys' and expert witness fees) reasonably incurred...."

42 U.S.C. § 5851(e)(2)

"The court, in issuing any final order under this subsection, may award costs of litigation (including reasonable attorney and expert witness fees) to any party whenever the court determines such award is appropriate."

Age Discrimination Act of 1975

42 U.S.C. § 6104(e)(1)

"Such interested person may elect, by a demand for relief in his complaint, to recover reasonable attorney's fees, in which case the court shall award the costs of the suit, including a reasonable attorney's fee, to the prevailing plaintiff."

National Oil Heat Research Alliance Act of 2000

42 U.S.C. § 6201 note (P.L. 106-469, § 712(e))

"(1) Meritorious Case — In a case in Federal court in which the court grants a public utility injunctive relief under subsection (d), the public utility shall be entitled to recover an attorney's fee from the Alliance and any qualified State association undertaking the consumer education activity with respect to which a complaint under this section is made.

(2) Non-meritorious Case — In any case under subsection (d) in which the court determines a complaint under subsection (b) to be frivolous and without merit, the prevailing party shall be entitled to recover an attorney's fee.

Energy Policy and Conservation Act

42 U.S.C. § 6305(d)

"The court, in issuing any final order in any action brought pursuant to subsection (a) of this section, may award costs of litigation (including reasonable attorney and expert witness fees) to any party, whenever the court determines such award is appropriate."

Solid Waste Disposal Act

42 U.S.C. § 6971(c)

"[A] sum equal to the aggregate amount of all costs and expenses (including attorney's fees)... shall be assessed against the person committing such violation."

42 U.S.C. § 6972(e)

"The court, in issuing any final order in any action brought pursuant to this section or section 7006 [42 U.S.C. § 6976], may award costs of litigation (including reasonable attorney and expert witness fees) to the prevailing or substantially prevailing party, whenever the court determines that such award is appropriate."

Clean Air Act

42 U.S.C. § 7413(b)

"In the case of any action brought by the Administrator under this subsection, the court may award costs of litigation (including reasonable attorney and expert witness fees) to the party or parties against whom such action was brought in any case where the court finds that such action was unreasonable."

42 U.S.C. § 7524(c)(6)

"Any person who fails to pay on a timely basis the amount of an assessment of a civil penalty as described in the first sentence of this paragraph shall be required to pay, in addition to that amount and interest, the United States' enforcement expenses, including attorneys fees and costs for collection proceedings...."

42 U.S.C. § 7604(d)

"The court, in issuing any final order in any action brought pursuant to subsection (a) of this section, may award costs of litigation (including reasonable attorney and expert witness fees) to any party, whenever the court determines such award is appropriate."

42 U.S.C. § 7607(f)

"In any judicial proceeding under this section, the court may award costs of litigation (including reasonable attorney and expert witness fees) whenever it determines that such award is appropriate."

42 U.S.C. § 7622(b)(2)(B)

"If an order is issued under this paragraph, the Secretary, at the request of the complainant, shall assess against the person against whom the order is issued a sum equal to the aggregate amount of costs and expenses (including attorneys' and expert witness fees) reasonably incurred...."

42 U.S.C. § 7622(e)(2)

"The court, in issuing any final order under this subsection, may award costs of litigation (including reasonable attorney and expert witness fees) to any party whenever the court determines such award is appropriate."

Power Plant and Industrial Fuel Use Act

42 U.S.C. § 8435(d)

"The court, in issuing any final order in any action brought under subsection (a) of this section, may award costs of litigation (including reasonable attorney and expert witness fees) to any party, whenever the court determines such award is appropriate."

Ocean Thermal Energy conservation Act of 1980

42 U.S.C. § 9124(d)

"The court, in issuing any final order in any action brought pursuant to subsection (a) of this section, may award costs of litigation (including reasonable attorney and expert witness fees) to any party whenever the court determines that such an award is appropriate."

Comprehensive Environmental Response, compensation, and Liability Act

42 U.S.C. § 9606(b)(2)(E)

"Reimbursement awarded by a court under subparagraph (C) or (D) may include appropriate costs, fees, and other expenses in accordance with subsections (a) and (d) of section 2412 of title 28 of the United States Code."

42 U.S.C. § 9610(c)

"Whenever an order is issued under this section to abate such violation, at the request of the applicant a sum equal to the aggregate amount of all costs and expenses (including the attorney's fees)... shall be assessed against the person committing such violation."

42 U.S.C. § 9612(c)(3)

"Upon the request of the President, the Attorney General shall commence an action on behalf of the [Hazardous Substance Response] Fund to recover any compensation paid by the Fund to any claimant pursuant to this subchapter, and, without regard to any limitation of liability, all interest, administrative and adjudicative costs, and attorney's fees incurred by the Fund by reason of the claim...."

42 U.S.C. § 9622(h)(3)

"If any person fails to pay a claim that has been settled under this subsection, the department or agency head shall request the Attorney General to bring a civil action in an appropriate district court to recover the amount of such claim plus costs, attorneys' fees, and interest from the date of the settlement."

42 U.S.C. § 9659(f)

"The court, in issuing any final order in any action brought pursuant to this section, may award costs of litigation (including reasonable attorney and expert witness fees) to the prevailing or the substantially prevailing party whenever the court determines such an award is appropriate."

42 U.S.C. § 11046(f)

"The court, in issuing any final order in any action brought pursuant to this section, may award costs of litigation (including reasonable attorney and expert witness fees) to the prevailing or the substantially prevailing party whenever the court determines such an award is appropriate."

Health Care Quality Improvement Act of 1986

42 U.S.C. § 11113

"[T]he court shall award to a substantially prevailing party defending against any such claim the cost of the suit attributable to such claim, including a reasonable attorney's fee, if the claim, or the claimant's conduct during the litigation of the claim, was frivolous, unreasonable, without foundation, or in bad faith...."

International child Abduction Remedies Act

42 U.S.C. § 11607(b)(3)

"Any court ordering the return of a child pursuant to an action brought under section 11603 of this title shall order the respondent to pay necessary expenses incurred by or on behalf of the petitioner, including court costs, legal fees... unless the respondent establishes that such order would be clearly inappropriate."

Americans with Disabilities Act

42 U.S.C. § 12205

"In any action or administrative proceeding commenced pursuant to this Act, the court or agency, in its discretion, may allow the prevailing party, other than the United States, a reasonable attorney's fee, including litigation expenses, and costs, and the United States shall be liable for the foregoing the same as a private individual."

National and Community Service Act of 1990

42 U.S.C. § 1263 6(f)(4)((D)(ii)

"If a participant, labor organization, or other interested individual described in paragraph (1) prevails under a binding arbitration proceeding, the State or local applicant described in paragraph (1) that is a party to such grievance shall pay the total cost of such proceeding and the attorneys' fees of such participant, labor organization, or individual, as the case may be."

Homeownership and Opportunity through HOPE Act

42 U.S.C. § 12875(e) *(see also,* 42 U.S.C. § 1437aaa-4(h))

"The parties specified in the preceding sentence shall be entitled to reasonable attorney fees upon prevailing in any such judicial action."

42 U.S.C. § 12895(d)

"The parties specified in the preceding sentence shall be entitled to reasonable attorney fees upon prevailing in any such judicial action."

Outer Continental Shelf Lands Act

43 U.S.C. § 1349(a)(5) (*see also,* 43 U.S.C. § 1845(e))

"A court, in issuing any final order many action brought pursuant to subsection (a)(1) or subsection (c) of this section, may award costs of litigation, including reasonable attorney and expert witness fees, to any party, whenever such court determines such award is appropriate."

43 U.S.C. § 1349(b)(2)

"Any resident of the United States who is injured in any manner through the failure of any operator to comply with any rule, regulation, order, or permit issued pursuant to this Act may bring an action for damages (including reasonable attorney fee and expert witness fees)...."

Alaska Native Claims Settlement Act

43 U.S.C. § 1619(b)

"A claim for attorney and consultant fees and out-of-pocket expenses may be submitted to the Chief Commissioner of the United States Court of Claims for services rendered before December 18, 1971 to any Native tribe...."

Alaska National Interest Lands Conservation Act

43 U.S.C. § 1631(c)(3) (*see also,* 16 U.S.C. § 3117(a))

"If title to land conveyed to a Native Corporation pursuant to the Alaska Native Claims Settlement Act or this Act which underlies a lake, river, or stream is challenged in a court of competent jurisdiction and such court determines that such land is owned by the Native Corporation, the Native Corporation shall be awarded a money judgment against the plaintiffs in an amount equal to its costs and attorney's fees, including costs and attorney's fees incurred on appeal."

Outer Continental Shelf Lands Act

43 U.S.C. § 1845(e) (see also, 43 U.S.C. § 1349)

"If the decision of the Secretary under subsection (d) of this section is in favor of the commercial fisherman filing the claim, the Secretary, as apart of the amount awarded, shall include reasonable claim preparation fees and reasonable attorney's fees, if any, incurred by the claimant in pursuing the claim."

Railway Labor Act

45 U.S.C. § 153(p)

"If the petitioner shall finally prevail he shall be allowed a reasonable attorney's fee to be taxed and collected as part of the costs of the suit."

Commercial Instruments and Maritime Liens

46 U.S.C. § 31304(b)

"If the plaintiff prevails, the court shall award costs and attorney fees to the plaintiff."

46 U.S.C. § 31325(d)(3)

"If the plaintiff prevails, the court may award costs and attorney fees to the plaintiff."

Merchant Marine Act of 1936

46 U.S.C. App. § 1227

"Any person who shall be injured in his business or property by reason of anything forbidden by this section may sue therefor... and shall recover threefold the damages by him sustained, and the cost of suit, including a reasonable attorney's fee."

Shipping Act of 1984

46 U.S.C. App. § 1710(h)(2)

"A defendant that prevails in a suit under this paragraph shall be allowed reasonable attorney's fees to be assessed and collected as part of the costs of the suit."

Communications Act of 1934

47 U.S.C. § 206

"[S]uch common carrier shall be liable to the person or persons injured thereby for… a reasonable counsel or attorney's fee...."

Satellite Home Viewer Improvement Act of 1999

4 U.S.C. § 325(e)(8)(B)(iii)

"If the Commission determines that a satellite carrier has retransmitted the television broadcast station to at least one person in the local market of such station and has failed to meet its burden of proving one of the defenses under paragraph (4) with respect to such retransmission, the Commission shall be required to... issue an order, within 45 days after the filing of the complaint, containing… an award to the complainant of that complainant's costs and reasonable attorney's fees."

47 U.S.C. § 407

"If the petitioner shall finally prevail, he shall be allowed a reasonable attorney fee to be fixed by the court."

Cable Communications Policy Act of 1984

47 U.S.C. § 553(c)(2)

"The court may… direct the recovery of full costs, including awarding reasonable attorneys' fees to an aggrieved party who prevails."

47 U.S.C. § 605(e)(3)(B)

"The court may… direct the recovery of full costs, including awarding reasonable attorneys' fees to an aggrieved party who prevails."

Alien Owners of Land

48 U.S.C. § 1506

"[S]uch suit shall be dismissed on payment of costs and a reasonable attorney fee to be fixed by the court."

ICC Termination Act of 1995

49 U.S.C. § 11704(d)(3)

"The district court shall award a reasonable attorney's fee as a part of the damages for which a rail carrier if found liable under this subsection. The district court shall tax and collect that fee as a part of the costs of the action."

49 U.S.C. § 11707(b)

"The court shall award a reasonable attorney's fee to the plaintiff in a judgment against the defendant rail carrier under subsection (a) of this section. The court shall tax and collect that fee as a part of the costs of the action."

49 U.S.C. § 14704(e)

"The district court shall award a reasonable attorney's fee under this section. The district court shall tax and collect that fee as a part of the costs of the action."

49 U.S.C. § 14707(c)

"In a civil action under subsection (a), the court may determine the amount of and award a reasonable attorney's fee to the prevailing party. That fee is in addition to costs allowable under the Federal Rules of Civil Procedure."

49 U.S.C. § 14708(d)

"In any court action to resolve a dispute between a shipper of household goods and a carrier providing transportation or service subject to jurisdiction under subchapter I or III of chapter 135 concerning the transportation of household goods by such carrier, the shipper shall be awarded reasonable attorney's fees if...."

49 U.S.C. § 14708(e)

"In any court action to resolve a dispute between a shipper of household goods and a carrier providing transportation, or service subject to jurisdiction under subchapter I or III of chapter 135 concerning the transportation of household goods by such carrier, such carrier may be awarded reasonable attorney's fees by the court only if the shipper brought such action in bad faith...."

49 U.S.C. § 15904(d)(2)

"The district court shall award a reasonable attorney's fee as part of the damages for which a carrier is found liable under this subsection. The district court shall tax and collect that fee as a part of the costs of the action."

Transportation

49 U.S.C. § 30116(c) (motor vehicle safety*)*

"The action may be brought... to recover damages, court costs, and a reasonable attorney's fee."

49 U.S.C. § 31105(b)(3)(B) (commercial motor vehicle safety)

"[T]he Secretary may assess against the person against whom the order is issued the costs (including attorney's fees) reasonably incurred by the complainant in bringing the complaint."

49 U.S.C. § 32508 (bumper standards)

"The court shall award costs and a reasonable attorney's fee to the owner when a judgment is entered for the owner."

49 U.S.C. § 32710(b) (odometers)

"The court shall award costs and a reasonable attorney's fee to the person when a judgment is entered for that person."

49 U.S.C. § 42121(b)(3)(C) (whistleblower protection)

"If the Secretary of Labor finds that a complaint under paragraph (1) is frivolous or has been brought in bad faith, the Secretary of Labor may award to the prevailing employer a reasonable attorney's fee not exceeding $1,000."

49 U.S.C. § 42121(b)(6)(B)

"The court, in issuing any final order under this paragraph, may award costs of litigation (including reasonable attorney and expert witness fees) to any party whenever the court determines such award is appropriate."

49 U.S.C. § 60121(b) (pipelines)

"The court may award costs, reasonable expert witness fees, and a reasonable attorney's fee to a prevailing plaintiff in an action under this section. The court may award costs to a prevailing defendant when the action is unreasonable, frivolous, or meritless."

49 U.S.C. § 80114(a) (lost stolen and destroyed negotiable bills)

"The court may order payment of reasonable costs and attorney's fees to the carrier."

Foreign Intelligence Surveillance Act of 1978

50 U.S.C. § 1810

"An aggrieved person... shall be entitled to recover... reasonable attorney's fees...."

50 U.S.C. § 1828

"An aggrieved person... whose premises, property, information, or material has been subjected to a physical search within the United States, or about whom information obtained by such a physical search has been disclosed or used in violation of section 307 shall have a cause of action against any person who committed such violation and shall be entitled to recover — (1) actual damages... ; (2) punitive damages; and (3) reasonable attorney's fees and other investigative and litigation costs reasonably incurred."

BIBLIOGRAPHY OF CONGRESSIONAL PUBLICATIONS

Committee Prints and Reports

On the Civil Rights Attorney's Fees Awards Act of 1976

House: Committee on the Judiciary. Civil Rights Attorney's Fees Awards Act of 1976; report to accompany H.R. 15460. Report No. 94-1558. 3 p. (94th Cong., 2d Sess.)

Senate: Committee on the Judiciary. Civil Rights Attorney's Fees Awards Act of 1976; report to accompany S. 2278. Report No. 94-10 11. 7 p. (94th Cong., 2d Sess.)

Senate: Committee on the Judiciary. Subcommittee on Constitutional Rights. Civil Rights Attorney's Fees Awards Act of 1976; Source Book: Legislative History, Texts, and Other Documents. Committee Print. 313 p. (94th Cong., 2d Sess.)

On the Equal Access to Justice Act

House: Conference Report. Small Business Assistance and Reimbursement for Certain Fees; report to accompany H.R. 5612. Report No. 96-1434. 29 p. (96th Cong., 2d Sess.)

House: Committee on the Judiciary. Equal Access to Justice Act; report to accompany S. 265. Report No. 96-1418. 30 p. (96th Cong., 2d Sess.)

House: Committee on Small Business. Small Business Equal Access to Justice Act; report to accompany H.R. 6429. Report No. 96-1005, Part 1. 29 p. (96th Cong., 1st Sess.)

Senate: Committee on the Judiciary. Equal Access to Justice Act; report to accompany S. 265. Report No. 96-253. 28 p. (96th Cong., 1st Sess.)

Senate: Committee on the Judiciary. Department of Justice Authorization Act, Fiscal Year 1981; report to accompany S. 2377 (incorporates S. 265). Report No. 96-786. 34 p. (96th Cong., 2d Sess.)

House: Committee on the Judiciary. Equal Access to Justice Act Amendments; report to accompany H.R. 5479. Report No. 98-992. 26 p. (98th Cong., 2d Sess.)

Senate: Committee on the Judiciary. Equal Access to Justice Act; report to accompany S. 919. Report No. 98-586. 39 p. (98th Cong., 2d Sess.)

House: Committee on the Judiciary. Equal Access to Justice Act Amendments; report to accompany H.R. 2378. Report No. 99-120. 30 p.; Part 2. 7 p. (99th Cong., 1st Sess.)

On Awards of Attorney's Fees in Tax Cases

House: Committee on Ways and Means. Subcommittee on Select Revenue Measures. Description of Laws and Bills Relating to Awards of Attorney's Fees in Tax Cases (Public Law 96-481, H.R. 1095, H.R. 2555, and H.R.3262). Joint Committee Print. 10 p. (97th Cong., 1st Sess.)

Senate: Committee on Finance. Subcommittee on Oversight of the Internal Revenue Service. Description of S. 1444 Relating to Awards of Attorney's Fees in Tax Cases. Joint Committee Print. 4 p. (95th Cong., 1st Sess.)

On the Handicapped Children's Protection Act of 1985

House: Committee on Education and Labor. Handicapped Children's Protection Act of 1985; report to accompany H.R. 1523. Report No. 99-296. 18 p. (99th Cong.. 1st Sess.)

Senate: Committee on Labor and Human Resources. Handicapped Children's Protection Act of 1985; report to accompany S. 415. Report No. 99-112. 18 p. (99th Cong., 1st Sess.)

House: Conference Report. Handicapped Children's Protection Act of 1986; report to accompany S. 415. Report No. 99-687. 8 p. (99th Cong., 2d Sess.)

On Funding of Participants in Agency Proceedings

House: Committee on the Judiciary. Regulation Reform Act of 1980; report together with supplemental and dissenting views to accompany H.R. 3263. Report No. 96-1393. (96th Cong.. 2d Sess.)

Senate: Committee on Commerce Agency Comments on the Payment of Reasonable Fees for Public Participation in Agency Proceedings. Committee Print. 75 p. (95th Cong., 1st Sess.)

Senate: Committee on Governmental Affairs. Study of Federal Regulation, Vol.111. Public Participation it Regulatory Agency Proceedings. Document No. 95-71. 162 p. (95th Cong., 1st Sess.)

Senate: Committee on the Judiciary. Participation in Government Proceedings Act of 1976; report together with minority views to accompany S.2715. Report No. 94-863. 52 p. (94th Cong., 2d Sess.)

Senate: Committee on Governmental Affairs and Committee on the Judiciary. Reform of Federal Regulation; report together with additional views to accompany S. 262. Report No. 96-1018, Part 1. (96th Cong., 2d Sess.)

On Attorneys' Fees Limitations

House: Committee on Veterans' Affairs. Legislative History of the Ten Dollar Attorney Fee Limitation in Claims for Veterans' Benefits. House Committee Print No. 8. 16 p. (100th Cong., 1st Sess.)

On Attorney Accountability Act of 1995

House: Committee on the Judiciary. Attorney Accountability Act of 1995. House Report 104-62. 34 p. (104th Cong., 1st Sess.)

Committee Hearings

House: Committee on Education and Labor. Subcommittee on Select Education. Handicapped Children's Protection Act. Hearings on H.R. 1523. 67 p. Mar. 12, 1985 (99th Cong., 1st Sess.)

House: Committee on the Judiciary. Subcommittee on Administrative Law and Governmental Relations. Public Participation in Agency Proceedings. Hearings on H.R. 3361 and related bills. 728 p. Mar. 30, 31; Apr. 1, 27 and 28, 1977 (95th Cong., 1st Sess.)

House: Committee on the Judiciary. Subcommittee on Administrative Law and Governmental Relations. Waiver to Obtain Attorney Fee Reimbursement [to Anne Burford]. 55 p. Mar. 20, 1986 (99th Cong., 2d Sess.)

House: Committee on the Judiciary. Subcommittee on Courts and Intellectual Property. Attorney Accountability. 294 p. Feb. 6 and 10, 1995 (104th Cong., 1st Sess.)

House: Committee on the Judiciary. Subcommittee on Courts, Civil Liberties, and the Administration of Justice. Awarding Attorneys' Fees. 426 p. Oct. 6, 8, and Dec. 3,1975 (94th Cong., 1st Sess.)

House: Committee on the Judiciary. Subcommittee on Courts. Civil Liberties, and the Administration of Justice. The Awarding of Attorneys' Fees in Federal Courts. 337p. Nov. 16 and 17, 1977 Apr. 26 and 27, 1978 (95th Cong., 1st and 2d Sess.)

House: Committee on the Judiciary. Subcommittee on Courts, Civil Liberties and the Administration of Justice. Awards of Attorneys' Fees Against the Federal Government. Hearings on S. 265. 629 p. May 20 and June 24, 1980 (96th Cong., 2d Sess.)

House: Committee on the Judiciary. Subcommittee on Courts, Civil Liberties, and the Administration of Justice. Implementation of the Equal Access to Justice Act. 302 p. Mar. 18 and Apr. 1, 1982 (97th Cong., 2d Sess.)

House: Committee on Judiciary. Subcommittee on Courts, Civil Liberties, and the Administration of Justice. Equal Access to Justice Act Amendments. Hearings on H.R. 5059. 413 p. Mar. 14, 1984 (98th Cong., 2d Sess.)

House: Committee on the Judiciary. Subcommittee on Courts, Civil Liberties, and the Administration of Justice. Equal Access to Justice Act Amendments. Hearings on H.R. 2223. 122 p. Apr. 30, 1985 (99th Cong., 1st Sess.)

House: Committee on the Judiciary. Subcommittee on Courts, Civil Liberties, and the Administration of Justice. Rules Enabling Act of 1985 [Rule 68 of the Federal Rules of Civil Procedure]. Hearings on H.R. 2633 and H.R. 3550. 342 p. June 6, 1985 (99th Cong., 1st Sess.)

House: Committee on the Judiciary. Subcommittee on Intellectual Property and Judicial Administration. Judicial Immunity Legislation. Hearings on H.R. 3206 and H.R. 671. 141 p. October 3, 1991 (102d Cong., 1st Sess.)

House: Committee on Small Business. Subcommittee on SBA and SBIC Authority and General Small Business Problems. Judicial Access/Court Costs —H.R. 5103 and H.R. 6429. 335 p. Apr. 17, 23, and May 1, 1980 (96th Cong., 2d Sess.)

House: Committee on Ways and Means. Subcommittee on Select Revenue Measures. Payment of Attorneys' Fees in Tax Litigation. Hearings on H.R. 4584 and Similar Bills. 111 p. Oct. 6, 1980 (96th Cong., 2d Sess.)

House: Committee on Ways and Means. Subcommittee on Select Revenue Measures. Payment of Attorneys' Fees in Tax Litigation. 100 p. Sept. 28, 1981 (97th Cong., 1st Sess.)

House: Committee on Ways and Means. Subcommittee on Social Security. Attorneys' Fees in Social Security Disability Cases. 299 p. May 13, 1987 (100th Cong., 1st Sess.)

House: Committee on Ways and Means. Subcommittee on Social Security. Processing of Attorney Fees by the Social Security Administration. 93 p. June 14, 2000 (106th Cong., 2d Sess.)

House: Committee on Ways and Means. Subcommittee on Select Revenue Measures. Award of Attorney's Fees in Tax Cases. 75 p. Apr. 25, 1985 (99th Cong., 1st Sess.)

Senate: Committee on Finance. Subcommittee on Oversight of the Internal Revenue Service. Taxpayer Protection and Reimbursement Act. Hearings on S. 1444. 192 p. July 19, 1979 (96th Cong., 1st Sess.)

Senate: Committee on Finance. Subcommittee on Oversight of the Internal Revenue Service. Recovery of Attorney's Fees in Tax Cases. Hearings on S. 752 and S. 1673. 173 p. Oct. 19, 1981 (97th Cong., 1st Sess.)

Senate: Committee on the Judiciary. Subcommittee on Administrative Practice and Procedure. Public Participation in Federal Agency Proceedings. Hearings on S. 2715. 905 p. Jan.30 and Feb. 6, 1976 (94th Cong., 2d Sess.)

Senate: Committee on the Judiciary. Subcommittee on Administrative Practice and Procedure. Public Participation in Federal Agency Proceedings Act of 1977. Hearings on S. 270. Part 1:745 p. Feb. 3, 11, and May 9, 1977. Part 2: 425 p. June 14 and 21, 1977 (95th Cong., 1st Sess.)

Senate: Committee on the Judiciary. Subcommittee on Agency Administration. Equal Access to Justice Act. 264 p. December 9, 1982 (97th Cong., 2d Sess.)

Senate: Committee on the Judiciary. Subcommittee on the Constitution. HUD Attorney's Fees. Hearings on S. 571. 117 p. Apr. 10, 1978 (95th Cong., 2d Sess.)

Senate: Committee on the Judiciary. Subcommittee on the Constitution. Attorney's Fees Awards, Hearings on S. 585. 127 p. Mar. 1,1982 (97th Cong., 2d Sess.)

Senate: Committee on the Judiciary. Subcommittee on the Constitution. The Legal Fee Equity Act. Hearings on S. 2802. 758 p. Sept. 11, 1984 (98th Cong., 2d Sess.)

Senate: Committee on the Judiciary. Subcommittee on the Constitution. Legal Fees Equity Act. Hearings on S. 1580, S. 1794, and S. 1795. 522 p. Oct. 8 and 29, 1985 (99th Cong., 1st Sess.)

Senate: Committee on the Judiciary. Subcommittee on Courts and Administrative Practice. A Judicial immunity. Hearings on S. 1482, S. 1512. and S. 1515. 291 p. Feb. 26, 1988 (100th Cong., 2d Sess.)

Senate Committee on the Judiciary. Subcommittee on Improvements in Judicial Machinery. Equal Access to Courts Hearings on S. 2354. 103 p. Mar. 13. 1978 (95th Cong., 2d Sess.)

Senate: Committee on the Judiciary. Subcommittee on Improvements in Judicial Machinery. Equal Access to Justice Act of 1979. Hearings on S. 265. 197 p. Apr. 19-21, 1979 (96th Cong., 1st Sess.)

Senate: Committee on the Judiciary. Subcommittee on Representation of Citizen Interests. The Effect of Legal Fees on the Adequacy of Representation. 1778 p. Sept. 19 and 20; Oct. 1, 2, 4, and 5, 1973 (93d Cong., 1st Sess.)

Senate: Committee on Labor and Human Resources. Subcommittee on the Handicapped. Handicapped Children's Protection Act of 1985. Hearings on S. 415. 115 p. May 16, 1986 (99th Cong., 1st Sess.)

House and Senate: Joint Hearing before the Committees on Veterans' Affairs. issues Arising in Connection with NARS v. Turnage. 424 p. Mar. 17, 1987 (100th Cong., 1st Sess.)

Chapter 2

ATTORNEYS' FEES AND LITIGATION EXPENSES IN SELECTED FOREIGN NATIONS

Sung Yoon Cho (Editor)

SUMMARY

This comparative summary is an overview of attorneys' fees legislation in fifteen countries — Australia, Canada, China, France, Great Britain, Germany, Greece, India, Italy, Japan, Mexico, Netherlands, Poland, Sweden, and Taiwan — based on country reports prepared by the foreign legal specialists responsible for these jurisdictions in the Law Library of Congress. The following aspects of the subject are treated below: (1) how attorneys' fees are regulated in civil litigation; (2) which party pays and/or how attorneys' fees or other litigation expenses are apportioned (this will be treated under the heading of liability for costs); (3) whether contingency fee arrangements have been adopted, and (4) what reform proposals exist, if any.

How Attorneys' Fees Are Regulated

All fifteen countries studied determine attorneys' fees in a variety of ways. In four common law countries, Great Britain, Canada, Australia, and India, courts are given wide discretion. For example, in Great Britain, under the Courts and Legal Service Act of 1990, the English courts are vested with the authority to determine by which party and to what extent the cost of litigation, including attorneys' fees, is to be paid. The court order for the payment of costs is reviewed by court officials, known as masters or taxing officers. Similarly, in Canada, under the Courts of Justice and Judicature Acts of Canada's provinces, the court awards the costs, including attorneys' fees, at its discretion, and its decision is later reviewed by taxing officers.

In the remaining eleven countries, attorneys' fees are regulated differently from country to country. The codes of Greece, Italy, Mexico, and Sweden authorize attorneys and clients to agree freely on the amount of attorneys' fees in accordance with the principles established in the codes' provisions. Both Italian and Greek legislation establishes minimum and maximum limits for the fees; while the maximum limit may be disregarded, the minimum fees are compulsory and any contrary agreement is void.

In France, litigation expenses and attorneys' fees are regulated by the New Code of Civil Procedure. It lists the following: the fees, taxes, government royalties, or emoluments levied by the clerks of the courts or the tax administration; compensation of witnesses; experts' fees; fixed disbursements; emoluments of public or ministerial officials; and attorneys' fees as required by law.

Attorneys in Germany are paid in accordance with a statutory fee schedule that takes into account the services rendered as well as the monetary value of the dispute, that is, the amount claimed. Therefore, a large monetary value means a large fee, even for indigent parties and even when negligible and simple legal work is required. Through so-called "fee units," the extent to which services are provided by the attorney is taken into consideration. The statutory schedule sets forth tables and rates that allow the determination of the fee unit for litigants whose dispute is valued at a given amount. Adherence to the fee schedule is not mandatory, as attorney and client may be allowed to agree on a different form of payment, but the court has the power to reduce exorbitant fees.

In Japan, attorneys' fees are governed by the Regulation of the Japan Federation of Bar Associations. The Regulation contains detailed statutory fee schedules. It lists seven kinds of attorneys' fees: initial retainer fee, success fee, service fee, counseling fee, opinion fee, regular retainer fee, and daily allowance fee. When a lawyer is first retained, the client pays an initial retainer fee (or commencing fee), with payment of the balance of the fee being contingent on the successful outcome of the case. Both fees are payable according to the fee schedule set forth in the Regulation. It is common practice among Japanese lawyers to use this unique "commencing fee plus success fee" arrangement. Several other countries, such as the Netherlands, Mexico, and Taiwan, attorneys' fees are also paid according to their statutory fee schedules.

Liability for Costs

With the exception of Japan, Mexico, China, and Taiwan, all the countries studied require that the losing party pay the winner's costs, including attorneys' fees. The countries may be further divided into two groups: (1) in the four common law countries, Great Britain, Canada, Australia, and India, the court is given discretion to rule on the allocation of costs on the basis of "the English Rule", as it is often referred to in the United States; (2) in the seven civil law countries, France, Germany, Greece, Italy, the Netherlands, Poland, and Sweden, their codes or statutes specifically prescribe that the courts will impose costs on the defeated party.

By contrast, under the codes or statutes of Japan, China, and Taiwan, the losing party is generally required to pay the litigation costs of the prevailing party, but not attorneys' fees. Each party pays its own lawyer's fees. In Mexico, the loser is required to pay the court costs of the successful litigant only in exceptional cases.

Common Law Countries

Under the English Rule, the successful litigant (the plaintiff or the defendant) is entitled to recover court costs and attorneys' fees from the loser. The purpose of this rule is to deter unmerited litigation. As was mentioned above, English, Canadian, Australian, and Indian courts have the authority to determine which party will be required to pay the costs of litigation, including attorneys' fees, as well as the extent of that party's liability for the costs and in what proportion. The court's discretion is subject to the rule that "costs follow the event," the event being success in litigation.

The British court's cost-shifting order is reviewed by taxing officers. In certain cases, the officer may not allow costs that are considered unjustifiable. This results in the winner recovering less than his full costs. However, litigants who receive legal aid, a program funded by the Government, are not subject to the English Rule. In Canada, the winner in a civil action pays a portion of his or her legal fees even though most of his or her court costs can be recovered from the losing party.

In Australia, although the English "loser-pays" rule is in use, there are significant differences in its application, in that the winner recovers less than he does in England. Moreover, in contrast to England, there is no publicly funded legal aid in Australia. In India, the winning party is entitled to costs unless he is guilty of misconduct or there is other good cause for not awarding costs to him. The general guiding principles that the courts in India use in awarding costs are spelled out in more detail than those found in English law.

Civil Law Countries

These countries appear to have adopted a "European Rule" although there is no single precise rule that can be identified as such. Nevertheless, a general statement can be made regarding the cost allocation rules adopted by all seven European countries. Namely, (1) the objective fact of defeat is sufficient grounds for imposing the costs on the losing party, without requiring any subjective elements such as fault or bad faith, and (2) the winner is entitled to recover not only court costs, but also the attorneys' fees and other expenses from the defeated party (either the plaintiff or the defendant). "Defeat" means complete defeat in all major aspects of the case.

It is well recognized that the above rules are to be qualified by many exceptions, some of which are established by statute and others developed by the courts. A few exceptions to the "loser- pays" rule are cited in each country report. For example, in Germany, Greece, Italy, the Netherlands, and Poland, when each party prevails on some claims but loses on others, the costs are to be divided proportionately. In Italy, the judge may exclude reimbursement of costs incurred by the winning party if he considers these costs excessive or superfluous, and he may order that the losing party be reimbursed for part of those expenses.

In Germany, the attorneys' fees of the winning party are calculated in accordance with the statutory fee schedule and the defeated party will not have to provide reimbursement for any excess amount thereof. In Sweden, the court may order the winning party to pay the loser's costs when it is found that the winner has no cause of action and that the proceeding is adjudged to have been unnecessary. In Poland, the loser may be ordered to bear only a part of the litigation expenses or none at all in cases where he could not possibly have predicted the outcome of the litigation.

Other Countries

In Japan, China, and Taiwan, the losing party is generally required to pay the litigation costs of the prevailing party. In these countries, litigation costs do not include attorneys' fees; each party pays its own lawyer's fees. In Japan, in exceptional cases, the winning party may be ordered to pay certain expenses entailed by unnecessary procedural actions or by a delay in the proceedings caused by said party's failure to present a timely defense or a general disregard of deadlines. When each party prevails on some claims but loses on others, the court, at its discretion, may apportion expenses to the parties.

In Mexico, as a rule, the court costs and attorneys' fees are borne by each party. In exceptional cases, the losing party may be ordered by the court to pay the court costs of the winning party who acted in bad faith causing unnecessary costs for the losing party or if the winning party brought up a frivolous case.

Contingency Fees

In all of the countries studied, with only a few exceptions, the contingency fee arrangements of the type used in the United States are either expressly prohibited or considered unethical or against public policy. Greece is the only country where the contingency fee agreement is explicitly allowed under the Lawyer's Code, but the amount payable to the attorney is limited to 20% of the amount actually awarded. Any agreement exceeding the amount of 20% is considered void as to the extra amount stipulated.

In Canada, the traditional English Rule prohibiting contingency fees has been considerably liberalized except the province of Ontario. Despite the liberalization, in practice, the use of contingency fees is still restricted; however, even though fees based on a percentage of the amount recovered are usually forbidden, agreements to charge reasonable fees on an hourly basis are allowed. In Ontario, the Law Society's recommendation to repeal the rule prohibiting fees "dependent on success" was not accepted. Instead, contingency fees are allowed in class action suits only, and even this practice remains fairly strictly controlled.

In Great Britain, a government proposal that called for the introduction of contingency fees — in an effort to increase litigation opportunities for those who do not qualify for legal aid but who are not able to afford expensive litigation — was rejected. In Australia, the Law Reform Commission's recommendation to allow contingency fees in class actions was also rejected.

It should be noted that quasi-contingency fee arrangements are used in several countries. The Japanese system of "commencing fee plus success fee, mentioned above, certainly falls under this category. Australian lawyers are allowed to accept fees on "spec" (i.e., speculation) in cases where an indigent injured plaintiff has a strong case of winning. Under the "spec" arrangements, the lawyer will advance part of the litigation expenses and is able to collect a fee that is somewhat larger than the normal fee if the litigation is successful.

Other examples of the quasi-contingency fee arrangements should be noted: in Germany, under the new consultation fee system, a modest fee enables a client to assess his chances of litigation. In addition, legal insurance is provided for many households, and generous legal aid is also available to indigent litigants. In Great Britain, legal aid is available to about half of the population. Under the British system, a winning party who is assisted by legal aid can recover costs in the normal way. However, when the losing party is assisted by legal aid, the court usually awards costs in modest sums, resulting in a substantial tactical advantage for that losing party.

Reform Proposals

In England, after the proposal to introduce contingency fees was rejected, a draft rule was issued under the Courts and Legal Services Act of 1990 to allow higher fees according to a "conditional fee arrangement," an arrangement already in use in Scotland. The Japan Federation of Bar Associations has recently prepared a draft to overhaul its complex fee system as part of judicial reform, to enable the public to consult lawyers more readily. However, these reform proposals are not intended to revise the existing "loser-pays" rule and introduce the use of contingency fees. In conclusion, on the basis of the fifteen countries whose attorneys' fees systems were studied, it appears that the traditional practice of cost allocation (the "loser-pays" rule, without contingency fees — excluding Greece), subject to many exceptions, will continue to be the norm.

AUSTRALIA

Kersi B. Shroff

Costs of Civil Litigation

Loser-Pays

A rule of civil litigation in Australia is that "costs follow the event," i.e. the losing party is ordered to pay the winner's costs, in addition, of course, to his own costs.[1] This is the same as under the English "loser-pays" rule. In Australia, however, there are significant differences in the application of the rule. First, there is an absence of publicly funded legal aid in Australia, particularly for actions of personal injury. Secondly, under the method of assessment of costs, the winner recovers less than he does in England.[2]

Contingency Fees

The payment of contingency fees has traditionally been opposed in Australia.[3] One of the arguments against this method is that under a "loser-pays" rule, it would be unfair to an opponent of a contingency fee litigant to incur the risk of having to pay the higher costs of the contingency arrangement.

---

1 Julian Disney, *et al.* Lawyers 430 (1986).

2 John Vargo, *The American Rule on Attorney Fee Allocation. The Injured Person's Access to Justice,* 42 AM. U. L. Rev. 1567, 1613 (1993).

3 Disney, *supra* note 1, at 424 et seq.

In 1988 the Australian Law Reform Commission recommended allowing contingency fees in class actions.[4] The government, however, felt unable to support the recommendation, as stated by a minister in the parliamentary debate on introducing class actions:

> [We] have set our face firmly against some features of the American legal system, such as contingency fees, which appear from my observations over there recently, to drive the American legal system rather than the merits of the issues themselves.[5]

No provision on contingency fees was enacted in the rules allowing class actions.

Australian lawyers, however, are allowed to accept fees, in some instances, on "spec."[6] i.e. speculation. Based on interviews with Australian lawyers, John Vargo reports that in cases where an indigent injured plaintiff has a strong case of recovery, under the "spec" arrangement the lawyer will either advance a loan, or have the client obtain a loan from an institution, to meet the expenses of the litigation. If the client is successful, the lawyer is able to recover part of his cost from the damages awarded to the plaintiff. This results in the lawyer being able to collect a fee that is somewhat larger than the normal fee.

CANADA

Stephen F. Clarke

Liability for Costs

Under the Courts of Justice and Judicature Acts of Canada's provinces, the awarding of costs is a matter that lies within the discretion of the judges who conduct proceedings.[7] Following traditional English practices, the established general rule is that the successful party is entitled to recover his or her costs from the other party or parties in a civil case. An award of "costs in the cause" indicates that the successful party can recover his or her costs on what is considered to be a normal scale. In practice, the normal scale is usually between two-thirds and three-quarters of the costs actually incurred by a party to most types of litigation. Thus, the Winner in a civil

---

4 Justice D. M. Ryan, *The Development of Representative Proceedings in the Federal Court,* 11 AUST. BAR REVIEW 131, 139 (1993).

5 *Hansard,* Senate, Nov. 13, 1991, p. 3025.

6 Vargo, *supra* note 2, at 1615-17.

7 For example, *see* Ontario's Courts of Justice Act, R.S.O. ch. C.43, §131 (1990).

action will usually have to pay a portion of his or her legal fees even though most of his or her costs will be recovered from the other side.

In order to entitle a successful party to greater than usual reimbursement, a judge can award "costs as between a solicitor and client" or "costs between a solicitor and his own client." In the latter case, the lawyer representing the successful party will usually send his or her entire bill to the unsuccessful party or parties. In the former case, the amount of fees recoverable will lie between those recoverable on the normal scale and those recoverable on a "solicitor and his own client" basis. Awards of "costs as between a solicitor and client" or "costs between a solicitor and his own client" basis are usually made to punish a party for maintaining a frivolous action, asserting a wholly unsupportable defense, or engaging in misconduct.

In addition to having the authority to award costs on a normal or a higher scale, judges can also provide that there will be "no order as to costs." In such an event, each party to a civil action is responsible for his or her own attorney's fees. Canadian judges sometimes waive costs when they believe that the successful party or parties have been guilty of some dishonesty or misconduct. Canadian courts do not have the authority to order witnesses to pay costs.[8]

The Crown is entitled to recover its costs in the same manner as a private party.[9] Money recovered in this manner is paid into provincial Consolidated Revenue Funds.

Contingency Fees

Unlike the situation with respect to liability for costs, there has been considerable liberalization of the traditional English rules prohibiting contingency fees in all Canadian provinces except Ontario. However, even those provinces that allow lawyers to enter into contingency arrangements place restrictions on the practice. Fees calculated as a percentage of the amount recovered are usually prohibited while agreements to charge reasonable, hourly-based fees only in the event of recovery are allowed.

In Ontario, the Solicitors Act still prohibits practitioners from "purchasing any interest in litigation' or making payment of their fees "dependent upon success."[10] The Law Society has recommended the repeal of this rule respecting "champerty," but thus far the Government has only enacted a Class Proceedings Act to, among other things, allow contingency fees in class actions.[11] However, while it is allowed in such cases, the practice is still fairly strictly controlled. Solicitors are only allowed to charge "reasonable" fees calculated in accordance with rules that define the proper method

---

8 Orr v. Positano, 6 C.P.C. 276 (Ont. Div. Ct. 1978).

9 *Id.*

10 R.S.O. ch. S.15, §28 (1990), as amended by 1992 S.O. ch. 32, §26 and 1993 S.O. ch. 27, Sced.

11 1992 S.O. ch. 6.

for establishing "base fees" and "multipliers" in a given class action. The intention in drafting these rules was to avoid the situation in which lawyers would receive far more in contingency fees than they would have had they been paid on an hourly basis.

CHINA

Tao-tai Hsia and Wendy I. Zeldin

According to article 7 of the Measures for the Collection of Fees in Civil Matters (for Trial Implementation) [hereinafter Measures],[12] at the end of litigation the loser of the case must pay the litigation fees. The people's court will send a bill to the loser stipulating what kind of expenses are involved and the amount. When there is conciliation, a popular method of resolving disputes in China, legal expenses are to be borne by both parties. The amount of expenses to be paid by the parties is also to be mediated by the court (Measures, art. 7, para. 4).

The litigation fees apparently do not include attorneys' fees. The Measures make no reference to them, and in a major book on the practice of lawyers and notaries,[13] there is no mention of payment of attorneys' fees by the losing party, nor is there any information about contingency fees. This is the only information currently available from material in the Law Library's collection. Based on this information, it seems that in China the losing party does not pay attorney's fees, nor is any contingency fee arrangement allowed.

---

[12] Adopted by the 203rd meeting of the Trial Committee of the Supreme People's Court on Aug. 30, 1984. *See* ZHONGHUA RENMIN GONGFIEGUO ZUIXIN FAGUI DA QUAN [complete Compendium of the Newest Laws and Regulations of the People's Republic of China] 714-715 (Beijing, Masses Press, 1993).

[13] *See* ZHONGGUO FALǓ SHIWU DAQUAN [Compendium on Legal Practice in China] 1263-1378 (Beijing, Beijing Broadcast College Press, 1992).

FRANCE

Phuong-khanh Nguyen

Litigation expenses and attorneys' fees[14] in France are governed by Title XVIII of Book I of the French New Code of Civil Procedure (NCCP).[15] All costs relating to court proceedings, documents, and the execution of court procedures are specifically governed by articles 695-700 of the new Code. Article 695 lists the following possible costs that could occur in a trial:

1) the fees, taxes, or government royalties, or emoluments levied by the clerks of the courts or by the tax administration, with the exception of fees, taxes, and penalties which may be due on documentary evidence produced in support of the claims of the parties,
2) compensation of witnesses,
3) experts' fees,
4) fixed disbursements,
5) emoluments of public or ministerial officials, and
6) attorneys' fees as they are regulated by law.

As a general rule, the losing party has to pay for all court costs, unless the judge decides that another party has to pay for all or a part of the cost (art. 696 of the Code).

Attorneys' fees are, therefore, paid by the losing party or the party against whom costs have beet assessed. Further article 699 stipulates that attorneys and solicitors, in matters in which their representation is required, have the right to recover directly against the losing party (or any party that has to pay) the expenses that they advanced without having received a retaining fee. In this case, they may request that the amount they had advanced be deducted from the assessment of costs against the party who has to pay.

The party against whom the recovery is pursued may, however, deduct as a legal set-off, the amount of the payment to his credit.

Although there is reference to expenses advanced by attorneys in article 699 of the NCCP, these are not the contingency fees of the type applied in the American system. Conditions for the attorneys' right of direct recovery are also stated in many court decisions, e.g., an attorney or solicitor is al1owed to claim advanced expenses

---

14 It may be important to note that lawyers in the French judiciary system are divided into two groups: 1) the "avocats" who are the equivalent to attorneys-at-law in the United States; and 2)the "avoués who act as solicitors.

15 NOUVEAU CODE DE PROCEDURE CIVILE (Paris, Dalloz, 1993).

through this procedure only if his representation was required or such a claim was granted in the judgment of the case.[16] French courts have referred to article 1999 of the Civil Code in deciding that the right to directly recover advanced expenses will not affect the right of the attorneys or solicitors to claim their regular services fee.[17]

The law also indicates that attorneys, solicitors and sheriffs may be held personally liable for costs relating to proceedings, documents and the execution procedures instituted beyond the scope of their authority (article 697).

GERMANY

Edith Palmer

Attorney Fees in Civil Litigation

In Germany, attorneys are usually paid in accordance with a statutory fee schedule[18] that takes into account the services rendered and, whenever possible, the monetary value of the dispute. In a civil action for damages, the value of the dispute is the amount claimed.

The extent to which services are provided by the attorney is taken into consideration through the so-called fee units. At the trial stage, up to four fee units can be claimed, one each for the activities of conducting the trial, presenting the evidence, negotiating, and reaching a settlement. In addition, various expenditures can be itemized. At the appellate level the fees are somewhat higher.

The statutory schedule provides tables and rates that allow the determination of the fee unit for litigation's valued at any given amount. The lowest fee unit is Deutsche Mark [DM] 50 [U.S. $ 35) for a matter valued at up to DM 600 (U.S. $ 420). For a matter valued at one million DM (U.S. $ 660,000), the fee unit is DM 6,225 ([U.S $ 4,140]). If these fees seem low, it must be taken into consideration that reimbursable expenditures also add up and that German attorneys as a rule do not provide as much investigative work as their American counterparts.

---

16 *Id.,* art. 699, notes 1 and 3.

17 *Id* art. 699, note 4. Article 1999 of the Civil Code stipulates that the principal has to reimburse his agent for all expenses and advanced funds that were incurred during the performance of his commission and also for compensation for services in accordance with any agreement that existed between the two parties.

18 Bundesgebührenordnung für Rechtsanwälte [BRAGO], July 26, 1957, BUNDESGESETZBLATT [BGBl., official law gazette of the Federal Republic of Germany] I, p. 907, as amended.

The current fees have only recently been enacted in the course of a reform of attorney fees and court costs.[19] For civil cases with a monetary value, the new fees represent a 15% increase over previous fees. Aside from raising the fees, the reform brought only minor changes while retaining the system of the fee units and certain similarities between attorney fees and court costs.[20]

Adherence to the fee schedule is not mandatory. Yet, while the law allows attorney and client to agree on a different form of payment, this freedom is not unlimited. Fees that are exorbitant can be reduced by the court.[21] Moreover, the rules on cost awards (see below) and the prohibition of contingent fees also favor the application of the statutory fee schedule.

Contingent Fees

Contingent fees are discouraged, if not prohibited, by the Ethics Code of the German Bar,[22] and they are forbidden by case law. The abhorrence of contingent fees dates back at least to the 1920s.[23] In 1986, the German Supreme Court[24] reiterated the prohibition of contingent fees in a decision that was affirmed in 1990.[25]

The 1986 decision prohibits and nullifies as being against public policy not only agreements that make the fee conditional on the attorney's success but also agreements that express the fee in a percentage of the judicial award or other satisfaction obtained. The Court reasoned that such arrangements are irreconcilable with the independence of the legal profession and its duty to uphold the law. According to the Court, contingent fees might motivate an attorney to pursue his quest for a victory with unethical means.

German law provides various devices to ensure that litigants are not kept away from the courts by the prospect of having to pay attorney fees. One of these is the newly introduced consultation fee. For a modest fee, a client can asses his chances of litigation.[26] In addition, many German households carry legal insurance and generous legal aid is provided for poor litigants.[127]

---

19 Kostenrechtsänderungsgesetz 1994, June 24, 1994, BGB1. I, p. 1325.

20 W. Madert, "Die Änderungen der BRAGO," 44 ANWALTSBLATT 305 (1994).

21 BRAGO, § 3.

22 Whereas the Ethics Code categorically forbids the fee to be expressed as a percentage of the award or settlement, the Code appears to allow, under exceptional circumstances, a fee to be made contingent on the outcome. [Grundsätze des allgemeinen Standesrechts, *as reprinted in* J. Lingenberg *and* F. Hummel, KOMMENTAR (Koln, 1988), § 52].

23 G. Harstang, ANWALTSRECHT 502 (Köln, 1991).

24 Bundesgerichtshof [BGH] decision, Dec. 4, 1986 40 NEUE JURISTISCHE WOCHENSCHRIFT 3203 (1987).

25 BGH decision March 22, 1990, 44 WERTPAPIER-MITTEILUNGEN 1250 (1990).

26 *Supra*, note 3.

27 Zivilprozessordnung, repromulgated Sept. 12, 1950, BGB1. I, p. 533, §§ 114, et seq.

The Loser Bears the Cost of Litigation

In civil litigation, costs are awarded in each case by the court as a part of the judgment. Costs are determined in accordance with sections 91 through 101 of the Code of Civil Procedure.[28] As a rule, the loser bears the court costs of both parties and all the necessary attorney costs of the winning party. The latter are computed in accordance with the statutory fee schedule and any cost in excess thereof would not be reimbursable by the loser.[29]

If each party is only partly successful, then the costs are split accordingly. This rule discourages the claiming of larger damages than could be expected to be awarded, because the extent that the claim is denied, the claiming party is considered as the loser.[30] In torts actions, German attorneys carefully look for precedents on damages for pain and suffering, so as to avoid inflated claims.

GREAT BRITAIN

Kersi B. Shroff

Payment of Costs of Civil Litigation

English courts have the authority to determine not only which party will be required to pay the costs of litigation but to what extent.[31] The exercise of the discretion is subject to the rule that 'costs follow the event,"[32] and, in practice, the successful civil litigant is generally reimbursed by the losing party for court costs, and attorney's fees.

The "loser pays" rule, however, is not straightforward and the manner in which costs are calculated does not result in complete recovery to the winner. The reimbursement of costs is not subject to the principle of *restitutio in integrum* applicable to the award of damages. However, the perilous position of a losing party

---

28 A translation as contained in S. Goren, The CODE OF CIVIL PROCEDURE RULES OF THE FEDERAL REPUBLIC OF GERMANY (Littleton, 1990) is included as an Appendix.

29 l. Rosenberg, K. Schwab, *and* P. Gottwald, ZIVILPROZESSRECHT 478 (München, 1993).

30 A. Baumbach *and* W. Lauterbach, J. Albers and P. Hartman, ZIVILPROZESSORDNUNG 277 (München, 1993).

31 Courts and Legal Services Act, 1990, ch. 41, §4.

32 Rules of the Supreme Court (RSC), Order 62, rule 3(3) & (4).

must not be understated. In a high stakes gamble of "double or quits" a loser may end up paying a huge price for attempting to obtain justice.[33]

Taxation of Costs

At the end of a trial, the court normally makes an order for the payment of costs. In determining the amount of the costs to be reimbursed to the winning litigant, an elaborate system of "taxation and assessment of costs" has been developed.[34] A review is conducted by court officials, known as masters or taxing officers, who usually apply a "standard basis" for awarding costs between litigants. This basis is defined as a "reasonable amount in respect of all costs reasonably incurred," with any doubts as to their reasonableness being resolved in favor of the paying party.[35] Until 1986, costs were applied on a restrictive "party-to-party" basis under which only those that were "necessarily and properly" incurred were allowed. The use of this basis resulted in the winner recovering between 33 to 25% less than the costs actually incurred.[36] The present "standard basis" allows a greater recovery to the winner.

The recovery of costs by the winning litigant is further reduced under other rules of procedure. For routine matters, such as an action for a debt, the rules provide a fixed range of costs. These are all that the winner can recover. The taxing officer may also disallow costs that are considered unjustifiable. This ensures that the litigant who has been extravagant in pursuing his claim cannot make the losing party pay for the excessive costs incurred.

Apart from the merits of the case, the court may also use its discretion to award costs based on the manner in which the case was conducted. Costs may thus not be allowed to the winner if the court determines that he has unreasonably or improperly done or failed to do something or has wasted costs as a result of an unreasonable or negligent act.[37] A legal representative is also made personally liable for the payment of wasted costs.[38]

---

[33] Tim Cornwell, *Quayle Likes the 'English Rule' But Brits Have Their Doubts,"* 14 LEGAL TIMES 1,12-13 (No. 38, Feb. 10, 1992), reporting an English action for medical malpractice in which an award of $396,000 by the trial judge was overturned by the Appeals Court, leaving the victim's widow to pay the defendant doctors' legal costs of $144,000.

[34] RSC, Order. 62, Part Ill.

[35] RSC, Order 62, rule 12.

[36] JACKSON'S MACHINERY OF JUSTICE 451 (8th ed. 1989).

[37] RSC, Order 62, rules 10 & 11.

[38] *Id.* rule 11. The rule is applied in the case of extreme conduct: Chiesman v. Davy-Chiesman, [1984] 1 All E.R. 321.

Legal Aid

The source of financing of litigation has a bearing on the payment of costs. Legal aid, including assistance in civil proceedings, is available to about half of the population. In applying for legal aid, the litigant must show that his disposable income and capital does not exceed the limit set from time to time by legal aid authorities and submit evidence that he has a good cause of action. When a successful party is legally aided, costs are recovered in the normal way. When, however, the loser is legally aided, the order of costs made against him cannot exceed an amount which is considered to be reasonable under the circumstances, including the financial resources of all the parties and their conduct in connection with the dispute.[39] in these cases, the court commonly awards costs in modest sums, the effect of which is that a legally aided person has a substantial tactical advantage.

The legal aid scheme's wide net of eligibility is stated to cushion the impact of the English Rule. The English lawyer who lost the high stakes medical malpractice action cited in footnote 4 nonetheless stated: "Without legal aid, the system would be weighted disproportionately in favor of the defendants. If a legal-aid system hadn't been in place, maybe we would have gone in the American direction."[40]

Contingency Fees

The English Rule must also be viewed in the context of the prohibition placed on lawyers from acting for clients on a contingent basis. A number of reasons have been advanced for maintaining the ban on contingency arrangements, *viz*, a conflict of interest may arise if the lawyer has a stake in the outcome of the litigation, rendering him unable to provide impartial advice; a lawyer may be tempted to encourage the client to settle early in order to avoid bringing the case to court; and lawyers may concentrate on cases with a high nuisance value in which the defendants are likely to offer to settle the case. Experience in the United States is also thought to indicate that contingency fees encourage juries to award excessive damages and encourage litigants to pursue cases with little merit, leading to an explosion in litigation.[41]

A government proposal called for the introduction of contingency fees for reasons of greater competition among and commitment from lawyers and to increase the opportunity for those who do not qualify for legal aid, but are able to afford expensive

---

39 Legal Aid Act, 1988, ch. 34, §17.

40 Cornwell, *supra* note 4, at 13. For further American commentary on the English system *see* John Vargo, *The American Rule in Attorney Fee Allocation: The Injured Person's Access to Justice,* 42 AM. U.L. REV. 1567; Herbert Kritzer, *The English Rule,* 78 A.B.A.J. *54* (Nov. 1992); Phillip Figa, The *'American Rule'Has Outlived Its Usefulness; Adopt the 'English Rule,'* 9 NAT'L L. J. 13 (1986).

41 Lord Chancellor's Department, *Contingency Fees,* Cm. 571, at 1 (1989) (the Green Paper).

litigation. Following a debate, however, it was decided not to allow the arrangement on grounds of principle and anticipated "undesirable side-effects."[42]

The White Paper instead outlined a "conditional fee, on a speculative basis," an arrangement already in use in Scotland. The principle of this arrangement is that it is reasonable for a lawyer who represents a client on a speculative basis to balance the risk of losing the case and ending up with no costs by charging a higher fee if the case is successful. The increase is expressed in terms of a percentage of the normal fee, the rate of the "uplift" being left for determination by the Lord Chancellor. A draft rule was issued under the Courts and Legal Services Act, 1990 [43] allowing conditional fees, and conditional informed risk analysis of the claim before trial. An English barrister writes: "Why should the client... underwrite the risk of losing? It will be the lawyers who underwrite that risk. The quality of their risk analysis of the merits of the case will be central to their future solvency."[44]

GREECE

Theresa Papademetriou

Liability for Fees

Court costs are borne in advance by each party with respect to his own expenses. After the suit is terminated, court costs are allocated in the court judgment following the so-called "defeat principle" whereby the loser bears the other party's court costs,[45] including attorney's fees. Courts may, however, in cases of partial victory or partial defeat, depart from this principle by allocating the costs to both parties depending on the extent of defeat or victory of each party.[46] Courts may also depart from the defeat principle if they deem that there were reasonable doubts as to the outcome of the trial and in cases involving spouses or close relatives.[47]

According to the Lawyer's Code, attorney's fees are arranged by an agreement between the attorney and his/her client.[48] The Lawyer's Code also provides for a

---

42 Lord Chancellor, *Legal Services: A Framework For the Future,* Cm. 740, at 41 (1989) (White Paper).

43 Ch. 41, §58.

44 Iain Goldrein, Streamlining the System, 91 LAW SOCIETY'S GAZETTE 17 (Sept. 14, 1994).

45 Code of Civil Procedure, [hereinafter: CCP] *in* P. Raptarchis, 10 DIARKES KQDIX NOMOTHESIAS [Permanent Code of Legislation] 154,11(a). (looseleaf)

46 *Id., art. 178.*

47 *Id.,* art. 179.

48 Lawyer's Code, art. 92 *in* 6A Raptarchis, *supra* note 1, at *354(e).*

minimum level of fees that depend on the amount involved in civil litigation and the type of procedure. Any agreement to receive less than the minimum fees is void.

Contingency Fees

In general, contingency fees are permitted in Greece.[49] The Lawyer's Code explicitly provides that an agreement between the lawyer and his client is allowed in which the kind and amount of remuneration depend on the outcome of the case or of the business transacted.[50] It may be agreed that remuneration will be made by granting to the attorney a part of the amount recovered. Contingency fees may not exceed 20% of the amount actually awarded. Any agreement exceeding the amount of 20% is void as to the amount beyond the limit.[51]

A lawyer who assumes a case on contingency fees undertakes the responsibility to bring the case to an end. If he loses the case, he will not be compensated for any services rendered.[52] On the other hand, a lawyer is entitled to be paid not only upon a successful outcome of the case but also in case of an out-of-court settlement.[53] If there is a dispute about whether or not the case is won, the bar association upon application of the client or his lawyer may decide on the issue. There is no appeal to this decision.

INDIA

Krishan Nehra

Costs

A litigant's costs include not only court fees for filing documents but also fees paid to an attorney for conducting his case. Recovery of such costs, if successful, does not follow as a matter of course. In order for a successful party to recover the costs

---

49 A decision of Court of First Instance of Athens 4853/1991 is on point. In brief, the Court held that an agreement between a client and his lawyer for payment depending on the outcome of a trial or the outcome of work done or other condition without any payment until the end of the trial is allowable. [40 NOMJKON VEMA [Legal Tribune] 302 (1992)].

50 Lawyer's Code, art. 92, para. 3, *supra* note 1, at 359(e).

51 *Id.*

52 *Id.* para. 5. There are also court decisions to the same effect. For instance, Supreme Court (Areios Pagos) decision No. 1747/1984 *in* 33 NOMJKO VEMA [Legal Tribune] 1135 (1985).

53 Ch. Chrisanthakis et al. SYLLOGE NOMOTHESIAS KAI NOMOLOGIAS PERI DIKEGORON [Compilation of Legislation and Court Decisions on Lawyers] 947 (1986).

incurred by him, the court must order such payment. Allowing a successful litigant to recover costs is thus at the discretion of the Court.[54]

The court has full power to determine by whom or out of what fund and to what extent, such costs are to be paid and gives all necessary directions for that purpose. The fact that the court has no jurisdiction to try the suit shall is no bar to the exercise of the power to award costs.

As a general rule, the costs follow the event the event being success in litigation. However, if the court directs that any costs shall not follow the event, it must state its reasons in writing.[55] A successful party is entitled to costs unless be is guilty of misconduct or there is some other good cause for not awarding cost to him.

The following are the general guiding principles which the courts in India use in awarding costs:

- Costs shall follow the event unless the court, for good reason, otherwise orders. Impliedly, the successful party is entitled to his/her costs unless guilty of misconduct.
- If a plaintiff substantially succeeds, even though not successful in obtaining the precise form of relief prayed for, the party is entitled to costs.
- If an amount less than the claim has been decreed, the costs will be apportioned according to the amount of recovery.
- If a plaintiff succeeds partially but fails on the important issue, he/she may be deprived of costs.
- If both parties advanced pleas far in excess of their legal rights, each party will be made to bear his/her own costs.
- If a third party appears and defends without sufficient reason, the party must bear his own costs even if the plaintiff was unsuccessful.
- The court, in its discretion, may direct the parties to bear their costs in cases where an important issue of law is settled for the first time.

Contingent Fees

In the absence of any statutory schedule of fees, it is customary that the attorney fees are settled by mutual agreement and paid in the beginning before the attorney begins proceedings in the matter following the client's instructions. This precludes any interest that an attorney may develop in the success of litigation for recovery of his fee if it is not paid in advance. Moreover, it is incumbent on the members of the

---

54 THE CODE OF CIVIL PROCEDURE, Act 5 of 1908, § 35.

55 *Id.* § 35(2).

professional bar in India that they "shall not stipulate for a fee contingent on the results of litigation or agree to share the proceeds thereof."[56]

The payment of contingent fee may become an inducement to the lawyer to use unfair means to gain success, such as the coaching of witnesses. Charging a contingent fee is considered commercialism in the legal profession and any lawyer indulging in the practice is liable to be dropped from the rolls for professional misconduct.

ITALY

Giovanni Salvo

Liability for Costs

Attorneys and clients are free to determine the amount of compensation for professional services in accordance with the principle established in article 2233 of the Civil Code.[57] Only in the absence of such an agreement may compensation for services rendered be determined, according to a scale of fees prepared and updated from time to time by the National Bar and implemented by a Decree of the Minister of Justice.

The scale divides fees in civil, criminal and extrajudicial, and establishes minimum and maximum limits for the various services. While the maximum limit may be disregarded and higher fees may be charged upon agreement, the minimum fees are compulsory and an agreement to the contrary is void. This principle is rationalized by the need to protect the decorum and dignity of the legal profession and to prevent fees from being lowered beyond reason to secure clients.

In cases of contested fees, the local Bar may try reconciliation between attorney and client, and even determine the appropriate fee, but the final decision rests with the courts according to article 2233, paragraph one of the Civil Code.

The Italian Code of Civil Procedure[58] provides for payment of attorneys' fees, as well as judicial costs, by the party or parties against whom the judgment is rendered. All parties to the proceedings must individually bear advanced payment of general expenditures but are entitled to reimbursement upon conclusion of the judicial process.

---

56 The Bar Council of India Rules, rule 20.

57 CODICI CIVILE E DI PROCEDURE CIVILE E LE LEGGI COMPLEMENTARI (Piacenza, La Tribuna, 1990).

58 *Id.*, para 1.

An appointed counsel is entitled to petition the court to provide, in the same decision ordering the payment of expenses, for the settlement of unpaid fees and disbursements due to him and to other attorneys.

Courts have the authority to exclude repeated expenses borne by the winning party when such expenses are deemed to be excessive or superfluous, and to order the reimbursement of part of these expenses to the other party. Courts may also apportion the expenses, in part or in their entirety, among the parties.

Contingency Fees

Regarding contingency fees,[59] lawyers cannot, under sanction of nullity and liability for damages, enter into any agreement, even through an intermediary, with their clients concerning the property that is the subject of the disputes entrusted to them. Therefore agreements awarding lawyers parts of properties or rights which are the subject of a litigation and those awarding a percentage of the value of said properties are forbidden under Italian law.

JAPAN

Sung Yoon Cho

In Japan, attorneys' fees are governed by the Regulation Concerning the Standards for Attorneys' Fees (hereinafter referred to as the Regulation), enacted in 1975 by the Japan Federation of Bar Associations.[60] Each bar association issues its own fee regulation on the basis of the Federation's Regulation.[61] The Regulation consists of 38 articles and a table of detailed statutory fee schedules for civil litigation. The Regulation lists seven kinds of attorneys' fees: initial retainer fee, success fee, service fee, counseling fee, opinion fee, regular retainer fee, and daily allowance fee.[62]

Initial Retainer Fee and Success Fee

When a lawyer is first retained in a civil case, the client pays an initial retainer fee (or commencing fee) with payment of the balance of the fee being contingent on

---

59 *Id.*, para 3.

60 Regulation No. 20, Mar, 8, 1975, as last amended on Mar. 7, 1992.

61 Kotama, *Hoshu nado kijun kitei* [Regulation Concerning the Standards for Attorneys' Fees], 26 JIYU TO SEIGI 5 (July, 1975).

62 *Supra* note 1, art. 2.

success. Both fees are payable according to the fee schedule set forth in the Regulation. However, article 4, paragraph 4, of the Regulation provides that if payment of the amount of an initial retainer fee as prescribed in the Regulation is unreasonable in view of the prospects of the case, the client's economic situation, or other relevant circumstances, the retainer fee may be reduced and the success fee increased to a fair and reasonable amount, provided that the total amount of the initial retainer fee and the success fee in such cases do not exceed twice the maximum limit of the amount of the success fee referred to in article 18, paragraph 2 *(please see below).*

Article 18, paragraph 1, states that the initial fee and the success fee for a civil litigation case are calculated in the table bellow.

Article 18, paragraph 2, states that the amount of the initial retainer fee or the success fee set forth in the above table may be respectively increased or decreased by 30% depending on the nature of the case.

This unique "commencing fee plus success fee" system is a common practice among Japanese lawyers. The contingent fee system under which the entire amount of the lawyer's fee is based on success has not been adopted by the Japan Federation of Bar Associations or individual bar associations.[63]

Amount of Claim *(Yen)*	Initial Retainer Fee	Success Fee
For the part up to 500,000	15 %	15%
In excess of 500,000 up to 1 million	12 %	12%
In excess of 1 million to 3 million	10%	10%
In excess of 3 million to 5 million	8%	8%
In excess of 5 million to 10 million	7 %	7%
In excess of 10 million to 50 million	5 %	5%
In excess of 50 million to 100 million	4 %	4%
in excess of 100 million to I billion	3%	3%
In excess of 1 billion	2 %	2%

Despite the above fee arrangement, an attorney may, upon consultation with the client, receive a fee on the basis of the amount of time spent on the assigned case at the rate of a minimum of 5,000 *yen* per half hour with the client.[64]

---

63 Kiyoichi Nakanishi, *Bengoshi gyomu to honshu no meikakuka* [Lawyers' Business and Accurate Fees], 70 JIYU TO SEIGI 70 (Jan. 1985).

64 *Supra* note 1, art. 6.

The Loser Pays Litigation Costs

Under the Code of Civil Procedure,[65] the losing party is generally required to pay the litigation costs of the prevailing party. In exceptional cases, the winning party may be ordered by the courts to pay certain expenses entailed by unnecessary procedural actions or by a delay in the proceedings caused by said party's failure to present a timely defense or a general disregard of deadline.[66] When each party prevails on some claims but loses on others, the court, at its discretion, may apportion expenses to the parties.[67]

The Court Expenses

The scope and amount of the court costs are set forth in the Law Concerning Civil Litigation Costs.[68] Filing fees are paid by the plaintiff by affixing stamps in the statutory amount fixed by the Law to the complaint or other document that is filed with the court.[69] Counsel fees are not included in litigation expenses. Each party pays its own lawyer's fees.

Proposals

The Japanese fee system has been targeted for criticism on the ground that it is too complicated for the public to make an easy estimate of the costs. As part of judicial reform to enable the public to consult lawyers more readily, the Japan Federation of Bar Associations has prepared a draft revision of the Regulation. The Federations' subcommittee for studying fee regulations has also launched an overall review of regulations on current fee standards issued by individual bar associations. The details of the draft regulation is unavailable at this time, but it is expected that the revision will be passed by the Federation in March, 1995.[70]

---

65 Law No. 29, Apr. 21, 1890, as last amended by Law No. 30, Apr. 2, 1992, art. 89

66 *Id.*, arts. 90 & 91.

67 *Id.* art. 92.

68 Law No. 40, Apr. 6, 1971, as last amended by Law No. 72, June 5, 1992.

69 *Id.*, art. 9.

70 This information was provided by Mr. Tatsuya Sakuma, Legal Attaché, Embassy of Japan, Washington, D.C.

MEXICO

Norma C. Gutiérrez

Attorney fees can be negotiated and stipulated in a contract under the provisions of article 2606 of the Civil Code.[71] If the attorney fees are not negotiated and determined in a covenant, the stipulated fees designated in the statute on lawyer's fees[72] must be followed.[73]

A survey of Mexican sources revealed that there are no specific provisions concerning contingent fees between attorneys and their clients in this jurisdiction. Based on the general principle in civil matters that restrictions must be expressed, it may be assumed that contingent fees are allowed, since they are not explicitly prohibited.

The court costs and attorneys' fees in civil law cases are borne by each party. Each party bears the cost incurred by the actions he/she files. However, in his verdict, the judge can exercise discretion and order the losing party to pay the court costs of his opponent if the opponent acted with bad faith during the trial or made the other party incur unnecessary costs or if the opponent brought up a frivolous case. The losing party will also be ordered to bear the costs of the winner if he loses at the trial level and at the appeal level on the same grounds.[74] The payment of the opponent's costs does not include indirect costs incurred as a consequence of the trial but those costs that are necessary and proper to conduct the procedures[75] according to the law. The Federal Supreme Court has ruled that the payment of trial costs cannot be negotiated by contract.[76]

---

71 CODIGO CIVIL PARA EL DISTRITO FEDERAL EN MATERIA COMÚN, Y PARA TODA LA REPUBLICA EN MATERIA FEDERAL (59th ed., Mexico, D.F., 1991), art. 2606.

72 Ley Orgánica de los Tribunales de Justicia del Fuero Común del Distrito Federal, title eleven, chapter I, *in* (CÓDIGO DE PROCEDIMIENTO CIVIL DEL DISTRITO FEDERAL (hereafter CPCDF), (8th ed., Mexico, D.F., 1990).

73 *Supra* note 1, art 2607.

74 CPCDF, art. 140.

75 *Id.*, art. 138.

76 *Id.* at 158.

THE NETHERLANDS

Karel Wennink

The 1992 Rules of Conduct for Lawyers,[77] together with international codes of conduct,[78] govern the conduct of lawyers in the Netherlands. Chapter VI deals with the remuneration of lawyers. Some of the important rules with respect to the charging of fees are laid down in Rule 25. In making up a fee note the lawyer has to charge a fee that is reasonable, taking into account all circumstances. The lawyer has to set up an invoice in such a way that the client can see how much is charged as a fee, as disbursements, and as turnover tax. Rule 26 states that the lawyer has to advise the client as soon as the lawyer expects the invoice to become considerably higher than the original estimate.

The above rules have been worked out in the Calculation Scheme for Lawyers,[79] which is based on a formula. The basic hourly rate is determined every few years by an independent firm of chartered accountants. The number of hours spent is multiplied by the basic hourly rate. Added to this is the VAT (Valued Added Tax) and disbursements. The outcome is multiplied by special factors which take into account the circumstances of the case such as experience, amount of work involved, know-how, speed required, etc.

In case the fee note is disputed, the lawyer has to have the fee determined by the local Order of Lawyers. In that instance, the lawyer has to draw up the fee note in a prescribed fashion and has to submit the file together with the fee note. The outcome is either that the lawyer has to lower the fee or the fee is accepted. If the fee note is accepted, the client should in principle pay. If the client refuses to pay, the district court will ultimately decide the case.

Rule 25, section 2, states that the lawyer is not at liberty to agree to charge a fee only in the event that a particular result is achieved. This means that contingency fees or "no cure, no pay" is not allowed.

Civil procedures are conducted at the costs of the litigants. Generally, the losing party has to bear the expenses of court costs and legal assistance.[80] However, in his verdict, the judge can order the losing party to pay the costs of the trial including his/her own expenses and all or part of those incurred by the other party. The verdict

---

77 E.E.Minkjan, ADVOCATENWET, NEDERLANDSE STAATSWETTEN EDITIE SCHUURMAN & JORDENS, no. 39 (6th. ed. 1993), p 251.

78 International Code of Ethics developed by the International Bar Association and the Common Code of Conduct and Explanatory Memorandum Code of Conduct for Lawyers in the European Union.

79 *Supra* note 1, at 319.

80 Law of Civil Procedure of the Netherlands, Decree of Sept. 16, 1896, STAATSBLAD [official gazette of the Netherlands] 156, as amended, art. 56.

will determine the amount of the costs, and the court can decide that no one will be awarded costs to be paid by the other party if both parties were partly wrong and partly right. The court can also award a percentage of the costs to the winning party and a percentage to the losing party.

Costs deemed unnecessary by the court are paid by the person who incurred them. However, the provision allocating the court's expenses does not cover all costs incurred by the winning party. In practice, the successful party is granted only part of his lawyer's fees.

POLAND

Bozena Sarnecka-Crouch

Liability

Poland, like the majority of countries, rejects the concept that each party bears its litigation expenses no matter what the litigation outcome is. Contrary to the U.S., Polish law is based on the premise that parties are responsible for the outcome of the litigation and that the losing party should bear the expenses, whether it lost the case on substantive or on procedural bases.

The Polish Code of Civil Procedure[81] in its article 98, section 1, states that a losing party is obliged to return to the winning party all expenses necessary for vindicating and defending his rights (litigation expenses).

In case of a party represented by an attorney, litigation expenses include: 1) court fees; 2) attorney fees and expenses, and 3) costs and fees connected with the activity of a party.[82]

Necessary litigation expenses include fees of only one attorney[83] which are calculated on attorney fees defined by the Regulation of the Minister of Justice.[84]

---

81 Ustawa z dnia 17 listopada 1964 r. Kodeks postepowania cywilnego, DZIENNIK USTAW, hereinafter Dz.U., No. 15, item 113 (1965); amended: Dz.U. No. 27, item 157 (1974); Dz.U. No. 39, item 231 (1974); Dz.U. No.45, item 234 (1975); Dz.U. No. 11, item 82 (1982); Dz.U. No. 30, item 210 (1982); Dz.U. No. 5, item 33 (1983); Dz.U. No. 45, item 241 (1984); Dz.U. No. 45, item 242 (1984); Dz.U. No. 20, item 86 (1985); Dz.U. No. 21, item 123 (1987); Dz.U. No. 41, item 324 (1988); Dz.U. No. 4, item 21(1989); Dz.U. No. 33, item 175 (1989); Dz.U. No. 14, item 88 (1990); Dz.U. No. 34, item 198 (1990); Dz.U. No. 53, item 306 (1990); Dz.U. No. 55, item 318 1990); Dz.U. No. 7, item 24 (1991); Dz.U. No. 22, item 92 (1991); Dz.U. No. 115, item 496 (1991); Dz.U. No. 12, item 53 (1993) [The Law of November 17, 1964 The Code of Civil Procedure, hereinafter the Procedure Code].

82 Slawomir Dalka, SADOWE POSTEPOWANIE CYWILNE. ZALOZENIA OGOLNE I PROCES CYWILNY [Judicial Civil Procedure. General Rules and Civil Procedure] 45 (Gdansk 1992).

83 Procedure Code, art. 98, sec. 3.

The court decides the matter of litigation expenses in any final decision.[85] The court awards litigation expenses at the request of the party. The party may present the motion to award litigation expenses until the conclusion of a trial before the court issues final judgment. If the party does not submit the request, its right expires.[86]

When both parties partially lose and partially win the litigation, their litigation expenses are divided proportionally.[87] When both parties lose the litigation in equal parts, both bear their litigation expenses.[88]

In exceptional cases, when the losing party could not possibly predict the outcome of the litigation, the court may decide that the losing party bears only a part of the litigation expenses or none at all.[89]

In some cases, the losing defendant will not bear the litigation expenses if he did not give any reason for litigation and accepted the request at the first possible moment at the trial.[90]

Contingency Fees

Contingency fees are not permitted and attorney fees are based on the value — and not on the outcome — of the litigation.[91]

SWEDEN

Fariborz Nozari

Swedish provisions concerning attorneys' fees are stipulated in a 1963 Regulation on the Rules Governing the Swedish Society of Advocates (Bar Association).[92] The Regulation does not contain any provisions on contingency fees. However, it allows for the conclusion of agreements between the attorney and the client with respect to

---

84 Rozporzadzenie Ministra Finansow z dnia 4 czerwca 1992 r. w sprawie oplat za czynnosci adwokackie w postepowaniu przed organami wymiaru sprawiedliwosci [Regulation of the Minister of Justice of June 4, 1992 on Attorney Fees for Representing a Party Before Judicial Bodies, hereinafter the Regulation], Dz.U. No. 48, item 220 (1992); amended: Dz.U. No. 119, item 578 (1994).

85 *Id.* art. 108.

86 *Id.* art. 109.

87 *Id.* art. 100.

88 *Id.* art. 100.

89 *Id.* at 102.

90 Procedure Code, art. 101.

91 The Regulation, para. 10, sec. 1.

92 SVENSK FÖRFATININGSSAMLING (SF5) 1963:580, as amended.

the fees charged. In the meantime, since members of the Society of Advocates are under an obligation to accept arbitration regarding a fee, should a dispute arise concerning the fee, the board of arbitration is free to disregard an agreement, if such agreement appears to be incompatible with the legitimate interest of the client or his insurance company.[93]

Although there are no immediate plans for a major change in the above-stated Regulation, it has nevertheless been amended, and will be amended, as circumstances require. The latest amendments were made in 1993, when the categories of members to be accepted in the Society were extended to cover Sweden's obligations vis-à-vis the European Union.[94] An amendment was also made in 1994 concerning legal practices managed in the form of a corporation. The amendment stipulates that unless the board of directors specifically allows otherwise only members of the Society of Advocates can be partners in a corporation.[95]

As to the payment of the attorney's fee and litigation expenses, in principle the losing party must pay the winning party's court costs, which consist of all expenses incurred in connection with litigation including the attorney's fee.[96] There are, however, exceptions to the general rule. For instance, according to the provisions of Chapter 18:2 of the Law of Procedure,[97] if the only means by which a case could be clarified is through a court judgment, the court may decide that each party pays for his own expenses. If it is found that the winning party had no reason to litigate and the proceeding is adjudged to have been unnecessary, the court can decide either to require the winning party to pay the loser's costs, or to order each party to pay for his own court costs.[98] If the winning party could have proceeded with a simpler process in conformity with the relevant laws, his right to compensation will be limited to what he could have been entitled to in a simpler form of litigation.[99] If a case is dismissed, the party whose case is dismissed is the loser and must compensate the other party's costs.[100]

Finally, it should be pointed out that, like the above-stated Regulation and other laws, the Law of Procedure has been amended, and will be amended, as often as deemed necessary to meet the requirements of the progressive development of law in line with social development and the need for meeting Sweden's international obligations.

---

93 SFS 1989:77, amending the above-mentioned Regulation.
94 SF5 1993:1597.
95 SFS 1994:1059.
96 The Swedish Law of Procedure, SVERIGES RIKES LAG (1994), ch. 18:1, p. 849.
97 *Id* Ch. 18:2.
98 Id. Ch. 18:3.
99 Id. Ch. 18:3a.
100 Id Ch. 18:5.

TAIWAN

Tao-tai Hsia and Wendy I. Zeldin

According to article 78 of the Code of Civil Procedure of the Republic of China,[101] litigation fees are to be borne by the losing party. Litigation fees do not include attorneys' fees. The matter of contingency fees is not addressed in the Lawyers' Law,[102] but article 33 of the law states that a lawyer may not be assigned the right in dispute between the parties in a lawsuit. This would seem to indicate that contingency fee arrangements are not allowed.

Moreover, the lawyers' association sets the standard of how much a lawyer can charge in fees. Article 36 of the Lawyers' Law states that lawyers are not allowed to receive any compensation beyond the agreed amount neither in lump-sum payments nor in installments, that is in violation of the law or the charter of the lawyers' association. According to article 34, lawyers may not instigate any lawsuit or use improper means to solicit litigation business.

---

101 Promulgated on Dec. 26, 1930, and last amended on Aug. 20, 1990.

102 Promulgated on Jan. 11, 1941, and last amended on Dec. 10, 1984.

ATTORNEYS' FEES: SELECTED MATERIALS

Constance A. Johnson

Aranson, Allison F. The United States percentage contingent fee system: ridicule and reform from an International perspective, 127 TEXAS INTERNATIONAL LAW JOURNAL 755-793 (1992). JX1.T48

Dedingfield, David. The Contingency fee system in America, 143 NEW LAW JOURNAL 1670(Nov. 26, 1993). LAW PER

Genii, Hazel. Financing the claim, HARD BARGAINING: OUT OF COURT SETTLEMENT IN PERSONAL INJURY ACTIONS. (Oxford, Clarendon Press, 1987). 194 p. KD1954.G46 1987

Greiter, Ivo. HOW TO GET YOUR MONEY IN FOREIGN COUNTRIES: A SURVEY OF COURT COSTS AND LAWYER'S FEES IN 151 COUNTRIES. (Boston, Kluwer Law and Taxation Publishers, 1988). 253 p. K2305.G74 1988

Harper, Timothy. Bye bye barrister 76 AMERICAN BAR ASSOCIATION JOURNAL 58-62 (Mar. 1990). K1 .M385

McCrory, Daniel P. Reform of the English legal profession: an American 'S perspective, 134 SOLICITOR' S JOURNAL 819-821 (June 1, 1990). K23.04

Mclntosh, David A. Misapplication of common law? (Great Britain), 56 DEFENSE COUNSEL JOURNAL 331-334 (July, 1989). K9. N7469

Napier, Michael, and Armstrong Nick. Costs after the event (United Kingdom), 143 NEW LAW JOURNAL 12 (Jan. 8, 1993). LAW PER

Pfenningstorf, Werner. The European experience with attorney fee shifting, 47 LAW AND CONTEMPORARY PROBLEMS 37 (1984). K12.A9. Reprinted by the American Bar Foundation as No. 2 in 1984 volume of its RESEARCH CONTRIBUTIONS OF THE AMERICAN BAR FOUNDATION.

Scott, I. R. The Green paper on continency fees (United Kingdom), $ CIVIL JUSTICE QUARTERLY 97-103(April 1989). K3.192

Vargo, John F. The American rule on attorney fee allocation: the injured person's access to justice (U.S., U.K., & Australia), 42 AMERICAN UNIVERSITY LAW REVIEW 1567-1639 (Spring-Summer 1993). LAW PER

Wheatley, Derek, A Way to pay the piper (continency fees for U.K. lawyers are to be introduced), THE TIMES 27 (Aug. 17, 1993). NEWSPAPER

INDEX

#

A

B

C

D

E

F

G

L

M

N

O

S

T

U

V

W